Mieke Bal

NARRATOLOGY

Introduction to the Theory of Narrative

Translated by
Christine van Boheemen

UNIVERSITY OF TORONTO PRESS
Toronto   Buffalo   London

© University of Toronto Press 1985
Toronto Buffalo London
Printed in Canada

ISBN 0-8020-5673-3 cloth
ISBN 0-8020-6557-0 paper

Reprinted in paper, 1988, 1992

Narratology: Introduction to the Theory of Narrative
is a translation, revised for English-language readers,
by Christine van Boheemen,
of the second, revised edition of
De theorie van vertellen en verhalen
(Muiderberg: Coutinho 1980).

Canadian Cataloguing in Publication Data

Bal, Mieke, 1946–
  Narratology

  Translation of: De theorie van vertellen en
  verhalen. 2nd ed.
  Bibliography: p.
  Includes index.
  ISBN 0-8020-5673-3 (bound). – ISBN 0-8020-6557-0 (pbk.)

  1. Narration (Rhetoric).   I. Title.

PN212.B313 1985   808.3   C85-098936-1

NARRATOLOGY
Introduction to the Theory of Narrative

Revised and adapted especially for English-language readers, this work is a translation by Christine van Boheemen of Professor Bal's enormously successful *De theorie van vertellen en verhalen*. It offers an introduction to all the major elements that make up narrative and provides a comprehensive theory of narrative texts and a set of concepts that students and others can use as heuristic devices in their own reading. It is illustrated with examples from various literary and non-literary texts.

The theory is based on a distinction between the text (the linguistic structure and the different speakers involved), the story (the arrangement of the content in a specific manner), and the fabula (the structure of the fictitious or 'real' content). The fabula requires the analysis of plot, actors as related to plot, time sequence, and location. The story is concerned with characters as elaborated images of individuals, with space and its symbolic or representational function, with the representation of time, and with point of view, here called focalization. The textual level is considered as a type of discourse – narrative, descriptive, or argumentative – while embedded items may have a dramatic structure; the relevant distinctions here concern the identity of speakers and their involvement in the fabula.

Mieke Bal's study provides a systematic introduction to a subject that is crucial to a wide range of texts.

MIEKE BAL is with the Institute of Comparative Literature, National University of Utrecht.

Contents

Preface to the English Translation

This introduction to narratology aims at presenting a *systematic* account of a theory of narrative for use in the study of literary and other narrative texts. It does not provide a survey of the major different trends in the field of narrative theory. There are other books available that provide such a survey. The choice for a systematic, hence limited, approach has been made for the sake of understanding, of the possibility of exchange of opinions, and of emancipation from intimidation. A systematic account of one theory, which proceeds from definition, showing at every step its own structure and the necessity of its own phases, is easier for beginners in the field to understand than a plural survey of many different theories, involving names, terms, and, especially, heterogeneous arguments. For the same reason, names of predecessors have been reduced to the absolute minimum and, wherever possible, accounted for in special paragraphs at the ends of the chapters. The theory presented as a whole is also better accessible in the sense that whoever uses it will understand it the same way. This agreement of users has the advantage of a greater intersubjectivity. Teaching it becomes easier, learning it more feasible, because the risk of misunderstanding is reduced. Finally, the use of a method of analysis that every participant in a discussion can master helps students overcome the feeling of intimidation that a brilliant but unexpectedly structured interpretation by a teacher often entails. It is that feeling – the feeling that the teacher, while conveying the desire to master literature, may at the same time, by the very brilliance of his or her performance, intimidate – that brought me to the development of the present account.

Once I was able to use a theory, I noticed a progression in the quality of my interpretations as well as in my capacity to teach.

The preceding remarks lead to an instrumental view of theory, indeed of this particular type of theory. Conceived as a set of tools, as a means to express and specify one's interpretative reactions to a text, the theory presented here holds no claim to certainty. It is not from a positivistic desire for absolute, empirical knowledge that this theory and its instrumental character should be considered to have been generated. It is, quite the opposite, conceived as it is *because* interpretation, although not absolutely arbitrary since it does, or should, interact with a text, is in practice unlimited and free. Hence, I find, the need for a discourse that makes each interpretation expressible, accessible, communicable. Secondly, the tools proposed can be put to varied uses. I have myself used this theory for both aesthetic and ideological criticism, and found soon enough that they cannot, or should not, be separated. Hence, the need of more theory, beyond narratology: a theory that accounts for the functions and positions of texts of different backgrounds, genres, and historical periods. One need not adhere to structuralism as a philosophy in order to be able to use the concepts and views presented in this book. Neither does one need to feel that adherence to, for example, a deconstructionist, Marxist, or feminist view of literature hinders the use of this book. I happen to use it myself for feminist criticism, and feel that it helps to make that approach the more convincing, because of the features a systematic account entails, as sketched above. The scope of narratology, in my view an indispensable tool, is a limited one. No student of literature will escape the work or the options a good study requires.

The examples given are various. They come from different linguistic communities, including Dutch, my native language. Many Dutch examples have been replaced by others from more accessible literatures. A few, however, have been kept; they are provided with a short bibliographical note at the end of the book. Examples are drawn from different levels of aesthetic elaboration; not only from well-known literary novels but also from works of children's fiction and journalism; there are even fictitious examples. The latter form a series and gave me the pleasure of reversing the classic examples of sexual role-divisions in linguistic publications.

The date of appearance of this book is a statement on its place in the discussion of literary studies. It comes late, if one considers it a result of structuralism. Coming after the vogue of anti- or post-structuralist theoretical works, it aims at an integration of different types of theories, at showing the necessity of a rational critical discourse within whatever view of literature one may hold, and at pursuing steadily the study of narrative as a genre, which stretches far beyond literature in the narrow, aesthetic sense. Soon after its appearance in Dutch, Christine van Boheemen found it useful in her teaching of English and American literature. She undertook the heavy task of adapting examples to an international audience, and of translating it into English without any guarantee of publication. If it appears today in its present form, it is due to her generous and competent efforts, for which I want to express my deep gratitude. I also thank Jonathan Culler who believed in the enterprise from the start and encouraged me to pursue it, even when facing difficulties of sorts which I would rather spare the reader. The same holds for Henry Schogt and Paul Perron, loyal supporters in Toronto.

Nobody but myself is responsible for misunderstandings the theory presented here may provoke. Feedback of any kind will always be most welcome; it will help to increase the usefulness of the book for the audience it aims at: those who, beginners or not, share my interest in narrative as a mode of cultural self-expression.

MB

Narratology

Introduction

Narratology is the theory of narrative texts. A theory is a systematic set of generalized statements about a particular segment of reality. That segment of reality, the corpus, about which narratology attempts to make its pronouncements consists of narrative texts. One should actually be able to say that the corpus consists of all narrative texts and only those texts which are narrative. One of the first problems in advancing such a theory is the formulation of characteristics with which we can delimit that corpus. Although everyone has a general idea of what narrative texts are, it is certainly not always easy to decide whether or not a given text should be considered narrative.

If the necessary characteristics can successfully be defined, these same characteristics can then serve as the point of departure for the next phase: a description of the way in which *each* narrative text is constructed. Once this is accomplished, we have a description of a *narrative system*. On the basis of this description, we can then examine the variations that are possible when the narrative system is concretized into narrative texts. This last step presupposes that an infinite number of narrative texts can be described using the finite number of concepts contained within the narrative system. This book presents an exposition of a coherent, systematic narratology and of the concepts pertaining to it. Readers are offered an instrument with which they can describe narrative texts. This does not imply that the theory is some kind of machine into which one inserts a text at one end and expects an adequate description to roll out at the other. The concepts that are presented here must be regarded as tools. These tools are useful in that they enable us to formulate a textual description in such a way that it is accessible to others. Furthermore, discovering the characteristics of a text can also be facilitated by insight into the abstract narrative system.

The textual description obtained with the aid of this theory can by no means be regarded as the only correct description possible. Another individual may perhaps use the same concepts differently, emphasize other aspects of the text, and, consequently, produce a different textual description. If the description of a text is understood as a proposal that can be presented to others, the fact that the description is formulated within the framework of a systematic theory carries with it one important advantage: it facilitates any discussion of the proposed description. With this in mind, we can return to the question of the corpus of narrative texts. What does this corpus consist of? At first glance, the answer seems obvious: novels, novellas, short stories, fairy tales, newspaper articles, and so forth. But, with or without motivation, we are establishing boundaries, boundaries with which not everyone would agree. Some people, for example, argue that comic strips belong to the corpus of narrative texts, but others disagree. If these people hope to reach an agreement, they must first be able to explain how they have arrived at their decisions. In this case, the explanation is very simple. Those individuals who consider comic strips to be narrative texts broadly interpret the concept *text*. In their view, a text does not have to be a *language* text. In comic strips another, non-linguistic, sign system is employed, namely the *picture*. Other individuals, sharing a more restricted interpretation of what constitutes a text, reserve this term for *language* texts only.

As this simple example demonstrates, it is important that we precisely define the concepts which we use. A definition should be formulated so clearly that everyone who works with the concept shares the same understanding of the notion as it was originally defined. This ideal situation is sometimes difficult to realize as, for example, when the concept in question has been used so often that it has begun to lead a life of its own and is understood somewhat differently by every user. Such is the case with very common and seemingly obvious notions such as *literature*, *text*, *narrative*, and *poem*. If, when working with such a notion, one does not feel capable of decisively resolving the problem of definition, it is, of course, possible to use a definition that is valid only for the particular study (lesson, discussion, thesis, article, etc.) with which one is engaged. The readers must then decide whether or not they will adopt the definition for use in other contexts; at any rate, the concepts under discussion have been clarified. A disagreement about the status of comic strips would quickly be settled if the definition of a text were first agreed on.

As suggested above, presenting a theory about narrative texts entails defining a number of central concepts. Within the scope of this *Introduction*, then, a *text* is a finite, structured whole composed of language signs. A *narrative text* is a text in which an agent relates a narrative. A *story* is a fabula that is presented in a certain manner. A *fabula* is a series of logically and chronologically related events that are caused or experienced by actors. An *event* is the transition from one state to another state. *Actors* are agents that perform actions. They are not necessarily human. *To act* is defined here as to cause or to experience an event. The assertion that a narrative text is one in which a story is related implies that the text *is* not the story. If two terms clearly have the same meaning, it is preferable to discard one. What is meant by these two terms can be clearly illustrated by the following example. Everyone in Europe is familiar with the story of Tom Thumb. However, not everyone has read that story in the same text. There are different versions; in other words, there are different texts in which that same story is related. There are noticeable differences among the various texts. Some texts are considered to be literary while others are not; some can be read aloud to children, others are too difficult. Evidently, narrative texts differ from one another even if the related story is the same. It is therefore useful to examine the text separate from the story.

The example of 'Tom Thumb' can again be used to illustrate the next distinction, that between story and fabula. This distinction is based upon the difference between the sequence of events and the *way in which* these events are presented. That difference lies not only in the language used. Despite their having read different texts, readers of 'Tom Thumb' usually agree with one another as to which of the characters deserves sympathy. They applaud the clever boy and they rejoice at the giant's misfortunes. In order that Tom might triumph over his enemy, readers are quite prepared to watch unabashedly as Tom exchanges crowns so that the giant unwittingly eats his own children. Readers are, in fact, delighted by this trick. Evidently, this rather cruel fabula is presented in such a way in all of the texts that the readers are willing to sacrifice one group of children for another. When 'Tom Thumb' is 'related' in another sign system – in a film, for example – the same reactions are evoked. This phenomenon demonstrates that something happens with the fabula which is not exclusively language-related.

These definitions suggest that a three-layer distinction – text, story, fabula – is a reasonable basis for a further study of narrative texts. This distinction is the point of departure for the theory of narrative texts that is presented here. Such a distinction carries with it the assumption that it is possible to analyse the three layers separately. That does not mean that these layers exist independently of one another. The only material which we have for our investigation is the text before us. And even this statement is not correctly put; the readers have only the book, paper and ink, and they must use this material to establish the structure of the text. That a text can be divided into three layers is a theoretical supposition based upon a process of reasoning. Only the text layer, embodied in the sign system of language, is directly accessible. The researcher distinguishes different layers of a text in order to account for particular effects which the text has upon its readers. Naturally, the reader, at least the 'average reader' – not the researcher – does not make such a distinction. In this *Introduction*, intended as an instrument for examining texts, the theory is based upon the notion of distinct layers, a distinction that is necessary for text analysis. It is, therefore, inevitable that that which is in effect inseparable should temporarily be disjoined.

Within this framework, the following topics will be discussed. The fabula, understood as material that is worked into a story, has been defined as a series of events. This series is constructed according to certain rules. We call this the *logic of events*. Structuralists often work from the assumption that the series of events that is presented in a story must answer to the same rules as those controlling human behaviour, since a narrative text would otherwise be impossible to understand. If human behaviour is taken as the criterion for describing events, then the question immediately arises of the function of the instruments of action, the actors. Greimas' suggestion that the actors be described in relation to the events provides one possible answer to this question. However, neither Bremond nor Greimas takes into account two other elements in a fabula that are logically describable. An event, no matter how insignificant, always takes up *time* in reality. This time has a hypothetical status: in a fabula the events have not 'actually' occurred. Nevertheless, the time is often important for the continuation of the fabula and must, consequently, be made describable. If Tom Thumb had not had seven-mile boots at his disposal, he would never have been able to flee from the giant in time. The difference between the time that Tom Thumb needs to escape from the giant's grasp and the time that the giant needs to wake up is, in this case, decisive for the close of the fabula. Furthermore, events always occur *somewhere*, be it a place that actually exists (Amsterdam) or an imaginary place (C.S. Lewis' Narnia). Events, actors, time, and location together constitute the material of a fabula. In order to differentiate the components of this layer from other aspects, I shall henceforth refer to them as *elements*.

These elements are organized in a certain way into a story. Their arrangement in relation to one another is such that they can produce the effect desired, be this convincing, moving, disgusting, or aesthetic. Several processes are involved in ordering the various elements into a story. These processes are not to be confused with the author's activity – it is both impossible and useless to generalize about the latter. The principles of ordering which are described here have a hypothetical status only, and their purpose is to make possible a description of highly refined material in the story.

1 The events are arranged in a sequence which can differ from the chronological sequence.
2 The amount of time which is allotted in the story to the various elements of the fabula is determined with respect to the amount of time which these elements take up in the fabula.
3 The actors are provided with distinct traits. In this manner, they are individualized and transformed into characters.
4 The locations where events occur are also given distinct characteristics and are thus transformed into specific places.
5 In addition to the necessary relationships among actors, events, locations, and time, all of which were already describable in the layer of the fabula, other relationships (symbolic, allusive, etc.) may exist among the various elements.
6 A choice is made from among the various 'points of view' from which the elements can be presented.

The results of these several processes is a specific story which is distinct from other stories. I shall refer to the traits which are specific to a given story as *aspects*.

A fabula that has been ordered into a story is still not a text. A narra-

not all dir. sp, 'is narr

NR

tive text is a story that is told in language; that is, it is converted into language signs. As was evident from the definition of a narrative text, these signs are produced by an agent who relates. This agent cannot be identified with the writer. Rather, the writer withdraws and calls upon a fictitious spokesman, an agent technically known as the *narrator*. But the narrator does not relate continually. Whenever direct speech occurs in the text, it is as if the narrator temporarily transfers this function to one of the actors. When describing the text layer, it is thus important to ascertain *who* is doing the narration.

✓

A text does not consist solely of narration in the specific sense. In every narrative text, one can point to passages that concern something other than events: an opinion about something, for example, or a disclosure on the part of the narrator which is not directly connected with the events, a description of a face or of a location, and so forth. It is thus possible to examine *what* is said in a text, and to classify it as narrative, descriptive, or argumentative. The one question that still remains is *how* all of this is narrated. There is often a noticeable difference between the narrator's style and that of the actors. As a result of this strict division into three parts, a division based upon the three distinct layers previously discussed, some topics that traditionally constitute a unified whole will be treated separately in different stages of this study.

On the basis of what has been said above, it should now be possible to formulate more precisely those characteristics that can be instrumental in specifying the corpus of narrative texts, the corpus for which this theory should be valid. However, this presents problems. Ideally, the characteristics of narrative texts should be as follows:

1 Two types of spokesmen are to be found in a narrative text; one does not play a role in the fabula whereas the other does (NB: this difference exists even when the narrator and the actor are one and the same person as, for example, in a narrative related in the first person. The narrator is the same person, but at another moment and in another situation than when s/he originally experienced the events).

1st pers, 64

2 It is possible to distinguish three layers in a narrative text: the text, the story, and the fabula. Each of these layers is describable.

3 That with which the narrative text is concerned, the 'contents,' is a series of connected events caused or experienced by actors.

Together, these characteristics should produce a definition: a narrative text is a text in which the above three characteristics may be found. The third characteristic also applies, for example, to dramatic texts. The problem, however, remains that there are texts which display all three characteristics, but which nevertheless, on the basis of either tradition or intuition, are not regarded as narrative texts. This is true of many poems. *The Waste Land* by T.S. Eliot is one of the numerous examples. A poem such as this may be termed a narrative poem, and its narrative characteristics may also be narratologically described. That this does not often occur can be attributed to the fact that the poem displays other, more salient characteristics, namely poetic characteristics; Eliot's poem remains first a poem, and its narrative characteristics are of but secondary importance. Evidently, the characteristics mentioned above do not lead to an absolute, watertight specification of the corpus. This in turn implies that a narrative theory makes describable only the narrative aspects of a text and not all the characteristics of a narrative text. It is, therefore, impossible to specify a fixed corpus; we can only specify a corpus of texts in which the narrative characteristics are so dominant that their description may be considered relevant. Another possibility is to use the theory to describe segments of non-narrative texts as well as the narrative aspects of any given text, such as, for example, the above-mentioned poem by Eliot. The problem of specifying a corpus is then solved in the sense that the relativity of such a specification is clearly established.

A number of descriptive concepts are obtained from the development of the theory of a narrative system set forth in the preceding pages. These concepts make possible a description of narrative texts *to the extent that they are narrative*. Because the theory to which these concepts pertain is a systematic one, it is in principle possible to give a complete description of a text, that is an account of all of the *narrative* characteristics of the text in question. However, such a description would consume a great amount of time and paper, and would, in the end, be rather uninteresting. The researcher, therefore, will always make a choice. Intuitively, on the basis of a careful reading of the text, s/he selects those elements of the theory which s/he thinks particularly relevant to the text that s/he wishes to describe. S/he can then use this partial description of the text to help in making further assumptions about other aspects of the text. These assumptions can then be tested on the basis of other data. The textual description that results provides the basis for an eventual interpretation. In other words, it is possible on the basis of a description ('the text is so constructed') to attach a meaning to the text ('the text means this'). An interpretation is never anything more than a proposal ('I think that the text means this'). If a proposal is to be accepted, it must be well founded ('I think, on the basis of the data shown, that the text means this'). If a proposal is based upon a precise description it can then be discussed. The theory presented here is an instrument for making descriptions and, as such, it inevitably but only indirectly leads to interpretation.

1

Fabula : Elements

1 PRELIMINARY REMARKS

'Innombrables sont les récits du monde.' So begins a now-famous article by Roland Barthes that sparked off a series of new developments in the theory of fabula.

Despite their many different forms, the fact that narrative texts, recognizable as such, can be found in all cultures, all levels of society, all countries, and all periods of human history led Barthes to conclude that all of these narrative texts are based upon one common model, a model that causes the narrative to be recognizable as narrative. Since then, studies of the structure of this general model have been conducted in several different countries simultaneously, and these studies have produced a number of important insights with which many researchers more or less agree. These studies were often based, either implicitly or explicitly, upon two assumptions.

One frequent assumption was that there exists a homology, a correspondence between the (linguistic) structure of the *sentence* and that of the whole *text* composed of various sentences. A homology was also assumed to exist between the 'deep structure' of the sentence and the 'deep structure' of the narrative text, the *fabula*. There are not as yet enough arguments to underpin this assumption, and it has as many proponents as opponents. It is more probable that the correspondence between the sentence and the text, or between the sentence and the fabula, rests upon a common *logical* basis. The purpose of the comparison between the fabula model and the sentence model which will later be introduced is to expose the logical principles of construction familiar to us from sentence analysis. The comparison is intended as an illustration only.

A second point of depárture in the search for the universal model for fabula was also a homology. A structural correspondence was assumed to exist between the fabulas of narratives and 'real' fabulas, that is between what people do and what actors do in fabulas that have been invented, between what people experience and what actors experience. It is of course true that if no homology were to exist, no correspondence however abstract, then people would not be able to understand narratives. Two arguments, both very restricted in their validity, have been introduced against the postulation of this homology. Firstly, it has been argued that the difference between literature and reality has been ignored. Scholars accused Bremond of this error on the basis of the latter's 'logic of events.' However, they overlook an important restriction that Bremond makes: it is not a question of concrete identicalness but rather of similarity. Pointing out correspondences does not imply that absolute equality is being suggested. Another objection to postulating the above homology is that, in certain types of narrative texts – for example, fantastic, absurd, or experimental – such a homology is absent; in fact, these texts are characterized by their denial or distortion of the logic of reality. Apart from the (quantitatively) marginal position of such texts, this objection can be countered with the argument that readers, intentionally or not, search for a logical line in such a text. They spend a great amount of energy in this search, and, if necessary, they introduce such a line themselves. No matter how absurd, tangled, or unreal a text may be, readers will tend to regard what they consider 'normal' as a criterion by which they can give meaning to the text. Textual descriptions of the *Nouveau Roman*, for example, clearly point in this direction. In order to understand a text, some sort of logical connection is needed.

It is not necessary to arrive at a definitive answer to this question. Certainly, the fabulas of most narrative texts do display the above homology. Consequently, most fabulas can be said to be constructed according to the demands of human 'logic of events' provided that this concept is not too narrowly understood. 'Logic of events' may be defined as a course of events that is experienced by the reader as natural and in accordance with the world. The precise nature of this homology as well as the degree of abstraction at which the homology still

holds true in even the most unrealistic fabulas are still being investigated. For the present, this point of departure has one important consequence: everything that can be said about the structure of fabulas also
bears on extra-literary facts. Various investigators in this area even
refer to themselves as anthropologists or sociologists (e.g. Bremond and
Greimas). Consequently, everything that is said in this chapter should
also be applicable to other connected series of human actions as well as
to elements in film, theatre, news reports, and social and individual
events in the world. It would take us too far here to make a statement
about such fundamental questions; it is, however, useful to keep in
mind the fact that the theory of *elements* makes describable a segment
of reality that is broader than that of narrative texts only.

The material which constitutes the fabula can be divided into 'fixed'
and 'changeable' elements; in other words, into objects and processes.
Objects may be understood not only as the actors who are more or less
stable in most fabulas, but also as locations and things. *Processes* are
the changes that occur in, with, through, and among the objects; in
other words, the events. The word *process* emphasizes the ideas of
development, succession, alteration, and interrelation among the
events. Both sorts of elements – objects and processes – are indispensable for the construction of a fabula. They cannot operate without one
another. It is, therefore, only for clarity's sake that these elements will
be treated separately here.

2   EVENTS

Selection

Events have been defined in this study as 'the transition from one state
to another state, caused or experienced by actors.' The word 'transition'
stresses the fact that an event is a *process*, an alteration. This seems
easy enough to demonstrate. However, trying to establish which
sentences in a text represent an event is often extremely difficult. The
difficulty arises not only from the fact that many sentences contain
elements that may be considered processes, but also from the fact that
these same elements may often be considered processes as well as
objects, depending upon the context. Such a selection, if it is at all feasible, ultimately results in an enormously large number of elements. It
is impossible to work with so many elements; the relationships among
the elements cannot be described if the collection is too large to survey.

A fourth problem is that the elements can only be compared with one another – a step that is necessary if relationships are to be established – if they display at least some correspondences with one another. In the following paragraphs I shall successively discuss three criteria, each of which further limits the number of events to be investigated, and each of which further develops a different aspect of the definition of events given above.

First Criterion: Change

Compare these two sentences:

    a John is ill.
    b John falls ill.

The first sentence describes a condition, the second a change. The difference can be seen in the verb. Would it be possible to select events on the basis of such a simple criterion? For the moment, it seems more sensible to begin by examining the series of events in which sentence *b* might occur. Imagine that the preceding text segment read as follows:

    c John was cleaning his house.

John's illness interrupts his activity and, as such, indicates a change. But in that case, sentence *c* can precede either sentence *a* or sentence *b* equally well.

    d John was cleaning his house. John is ill.

is just as intelligible as

    e John was cleaning his house. John fell ill.

In both cases the cleaning activities are interrupted although in neither case is this *explicitly* stated. Sentences *d* and *e* differ in the same way from, for example, a text segment such as:

    f John was cleaning his house. John fell ill and therefore had to stop cleaning.

The explicit relationship established in sentence *f* is only implied in *d*

and *e*. The relationship between *c* and *a*, or between *c* and *b*, is decisive
for an analysis of the events; it is only in a *series* that events become
meaningful for the further development of the fabula. According to this
view, it is pointless to consider whether or not an isolated fact is an
event. The linguistic form in which the information is embodied can be
an *indication*, but it is not always decisive. Furthermore, the general
assumption that every event is indicated by a *verb of action* is also
unjustified. It is, of course, possible to restate every event so that a verb
of action appears in the sentence as, for example, with the verb 'stop' in
sentence *f*. This provides a convenient means of making explicit any
implicit relationships between facts, and can lead to a preliminary
selection of events. As a result, however, the number of possible events
becomes so large that another specific criterion for selecting events
must be found.

Second Criterion: Choice

In the previously cited article by Barthes, the author distinguishes
between functional and non-functional events. Functional events open
a choice between two possibilities, realize this choice, or reveal the
results of such a choice. Once a choice is made, it determines the following course of events in the developments of the fabula. This can be
illustrated by a simple example. Compare the following text segments:

g Liz leaves her house to go to work.
   She turns left and walks straight ahead.
   She arrives at eight-thirty.

h Liz leaves her house to go to work.
   She walks straight ahead, and crosses the street.
   Unconscious, she is carried into a hospital at eight-thirty.

Again, something is implied in both text segments: in *g*, that Liz successfully covered a certain distance; in *h*, that she was run down while
crossing the street. If, soon after eight-thirty, something happens at
work that influences the further development of the fabula, then the
statement 'she turns left' may be considered to constitute an event:
because the actor chose a certain route, she arrived in time to make the
following event possible. Should that not be the case, it does not mean
that turning left has no significance. It cannot be included in the succession of *functional* events, but it can point to some particular charac-

teristic of the actor in question. For example, it can indicate a punctual attitude towards work, a preference for a certain route, or leftish political views; this depends upon the network of meaning in the text as a whole. However, for the purpose of *this* analysis, namely the selection of functional events, this text segment may be left out of consideration. In sentence *h*, something happens that most probably has consequences for the rest of the fabula. The actor is run down, something that would not have happened if she had chosen the other route. In turn, the accident presents a number of alternatives. Was Liz hit intentionally or not? If so, by an acquaintance or by a stranger? Questions such as these could form the subject for a detective story. The sentence 'She walks straight ahead and crosses the street' indicates a functional event. But even if the result of sentence *h* is more spectacular than that of sentence *g*, this does not imply that such an event as that in sentence *h* always satisfies the criterion. If this text segment is unrelated to the rest of the fabula and refers instead only to the world in which the fabula occurs – the accident can, for example, illustrate traffic congestion during the rush hour – then the choice in sentence *h* between turning left and crossing the street is not a functional event. As with the selection in the previous paragraph, an intuitive decision is often necessary here. It is not always possible to point out formal characteristics of functionality. That an agreement may, however, be reached is demonstrated in the analysis that Chatman conducted using this method. The differences of opinion that may persist concerning some of the details of his analysis of a narration from Joyce's *Dubliners* do not detract from his textual description as a whole.

Third Criterion: Confrontation

A third criterion for selecting events has been suggested by Hendricks. In a programmatic article, Hendricks presents a promising method for extracting the structure of the fabula from the text via formal procedures. His method is very laborious and does not resolve all of the difficulties that still remain. Nevertheless, one of his most important points can help to formalize and further refine Barthes' method so that the results are less intuitive and the number of functional events is further reduced. Hendricks' point of departure is that the structure of the fabula is determined by confrontation. Two actors or groups of actors are confronted by each other. Although it has not been proven that this is true of all fabulas, it is probably possible in most instances to view the actors as two contrasting groups, provided that we keep in mind the fact that this division does not necessarily have to remain constant for the duration of the fabula. Every phase of the fabula – every functional event – consists of three components: two actors and one action; stated in the logical terms used by Hendricks, two arguments and one predicate; in yet another formulation, two objects and one process. Linguistically, it should be possible to formulate this unity as: two nominal and one verbal component. The structure of the basis sentence would then be:

subject – predicate – (direct) object

in which both the subject and the (direct) object must be actors, agents of action.

According to this third criterion, only those segments of the text that can be presented by such a basis sentence constitute a functional event. Rewriting text segments as basis sentences demands a bit of skill. Compare the following text segments:

i Liz writes a letter.

j Panting from exhaustion, John sat down. The entire room had been washed. He felt that he had earned a reward, so he poured himself a cup of coffee, dropped in two cubes of sugar, added a bit of evaporated skim milk, and took the most recent book from the *True Romances* down from the shelf. 'Great books for relaxing after work,' he said to himself. 'Not too difficult.' But the housework had been too strenuous, and he simply could not concentrate.

k John kills a fly.

l John kills a woman.

According to Hendricks' criterion, sentence i is lacking one component. There is a subject, a predicate and a direct object, but this last component (a letter) is not an actor. The necessary confrontation is, then, impossible. But writing a letter is an activity which presupposes an addressee. The letter is written *to someone*. Although the second actor is not specifically named in this sentence, his or her existence is implied. Consequently, sentence i can be rewritten with the help of surrounding text segments: Liz writes (a letter to) John (or, to the tax inspector, her employees, her friend). Because it is possible to rewrite the sentence in this manner, we may consider it relevant to the structure of the fabula.

This same possibility is not implied in sentence *j*. Despite the numerous actions performed by John, and the lifestyle which they suggest to the reader, John remains an isolated agent of action. His actions are not considered to be functional events because they do not bring about any change in the relation between John and another (group of) actor(s).

Sentences *k* and *l* share a common subject and predicate; both sentences can provide just as much information about the character of the subject, but the difference between the two is clear. Here again, the nature of the direct object *itself* cannot provide a definite answer. Again, the answer as to whether either the fly or the woman may be considered an actor depends upon the context. It is quite possible to imagine a fabula in which John is continually confronted by a fly, as in La Fontaine's fable 'Le Coche et la Mouche' for example; on the other hand, a murder can serve to illustrate a character trait and have no influence whatsoever on the development of the fabula, as in the short story 'The Man That Turned into a Statue' by Joyce Carol Oates. In this text, a woman who can in no way be considered an actor is murdered.

The results of an analysis according to Hendricks' method correspond strikingly with the results obtained from an analysis via Barthes' method, despite the fact that the former method is much more precise. Naturally, the relative importance of being able to formalize one's analysis depends upon one's purpose in conducting it. A very intuitive selection is often satisfactory, and a more formal method can be reserved for difficult decisions.

Relationships

According to the definition used in this study, a fabula is 'a series of logically and chronologically related events.' Once we have decided which facts can be considered events, we can then describe the relationships which connect one event to the other: the *structure* of the series of events. A method for obtaining this description is discussed in the following paragraphs. Starting from Barthes' assumption that all fabulas are based upon one model, we can begin to search for a model that is so abstract that it may be considered universal – until, that is, the model in question is either rejected or improved. This model is then 'laid upon' the text which is being investigated; in other words, we examine the way in which and extent to which the concrete events can be placed in the basis model. The purpose of this work method is not to force the text into a general model and then to conclude that the text is indeed narrative. Such a procedure could at best be useful for testing doubtful cases when trying to specify the corpus. Rather, a confrontation between a concrete fabula and a general model allows the description of the structure of the fabula of the text in question to be stated more precisely *with regard to* the basis model by which the specific structure is placed in relief and made visible. A 'perfect fit' as well as any deviations from the basis model can influence the meaning of the text.

One model which makes ample provision for this possibility is that suggested by Bremond. It must be remarked here that Bremond begins from the second postulate discussed in section 1, above: according to him, the narrated universal is regulated by the same rules as those which control human thought and action. These rules are determined by logical and conventional restrictions. A logical rule is, for example, that effect succeeds cause; thus, the hero dies *after* the bullet strikes him. A conventional restriction is, for example, that a worker is not rich. The two sorts of restrictions have to do with each other; conventional restrictions could be seen as the interpretation, by historically and culturally determined groups, of logical rules in concrete situations. Also included among the conventional restrictions are the traditional rules to which texts of specific genres must conform; for example, a classical tragedy takes place in the upper social circles.

As is true of every model, Bremond's model is abstract. This implies that he presents terms which can represent a large number of events; the events from every distinct fabula can be 'translated' into these abstract terms. In this way, the relations among the events can be made visible. The next section contains a brief reproduction of this model. This is then followed by a short survey of a few other principles for determining relations.

The Narrative Cycle

A fabula may be considered as a specific grouping of series of events. The fabula as a whole constitutes a process, while every event can also be called a process or, at least, part of a process. Three phases can be distinguished in every fabula: the possibility (or virtuality), the event (or realization), and the result (or conclusion) of the process. None of these three phases is indispensable. A possibility can just as well be realized as not. And even if the event is realized, a successful conclusion is not always ensured. The following example illustrates these possibilities:

> *a* Liz wants to earn a diploma.

The following alternatives are possible:

> 1 Liz wants to earn a diploma (possibility)

> 2.a She prepares for the exam (realization)
> 2.b She does not prepare for the exam (no realization)

In b, the cycle is prematurely completed; in a, the third phase begins:

> 3.a She passes the exam (conclusion)
> 3.b She fails the exam (negative conclusion which can lead to the recommencement of the cycle)

These phases cannot always be explicitly found in the text, as is demonstrated in example *b*:

> *b* John wants to offer his girl friend a lovely dinner. The beef Stroganoff tastes delicious. (The butcher was closed so John serves a sandwich.) (The beef was excellent but, unfortunately, burnt.)

The preceding has been an elaboration of Barthes' criterion for selection. Bremond calls this first grouping an *elementary series*. These series are combined with one another. The combination of elementary series into *complex series* can assume a variety of forms. The processes can occur *one after the other*. In this case, the result of the first process is also the beginning (virtuality) of the new process.

> *c* John is tired (= he can rest)
>   He rests (= he feels fine again)
>   He feels fine (= he can work again) = John feels fine (= he can work)
>   He works (= he becomes tired)
>   He is tired (= he can rest),
>   etc.

The processes can also be *embedded* in another process, as, for example, when one possibility opens another, or when one realization leads to another possibility.

    d John is tired (= he can fall asleep)
       John falls asleep = John can forget about his exam
                          He forgets about his exam
                          He fails
       John feels fine again.

In this example, the first series, the 'head series,' leads to an improvement in John's condition, and the embedded series leads to a deterioration. As is apparent from this example, the so called 'head series' does not have to be more important than the embedded series in order for the fabula to proceed; the embedded series is probably more important in the above example. Such data *can* lead to pronouncements about the 'style' of a fabula. When, for example, important events are continually embedded in everyday, banal events which are the cause of the important events, a certain effect is probably produced. It can, for example, be an expression of fatalism, of the impotency of man against the world, or of an existential view of life.
    In *d*, a *causal* relationship can be indicated between the head series and the embedded series. This does not always have to be the case. The embedded series often provides a *specification* of the head series.

    e Peter insults John
       John is angry   = John asks for an explanation
                                      Peter explains
       John is no longer angry   = John understands.

In this example, asking for an explanation is a specific form of being angry. It is also possible to express anger in another way, for example, by hitting someone; in this case, another embedded series with another specification of the head series would evolve.
    There are innumerable possibilities for succession and embedding, so that an infinite number of fabulas can be formed. Bremond's further structuring of these series is based upon his definition of narrative texts which is as follows:

    A narrative consists of a language act by which a succession of
    events having human interest are integrated into the unity of this
    same act.   (Bremond 1977, 186)

With regard to the fabula, this definition distinguishes itself from the definition given earlier in this *Introduction* only by the addition of 'human interest.' Because this difference is actually a theoretical one and will seldom lead to different conclusions, I do not need to discuss the issue further at this point.

One division between the processes is that between *processes of improvement* and *processes of deterioration*. Both sorts can become possible, both can be realized or not, and both can conclude successfully or not.

Example *e* represents a possible deterioration which is avoided by an embedded improvement. In example *d*, the process of improvement contains an embedded deterioration, while example *c* represents an improvement and a deterioration immediately following each other.

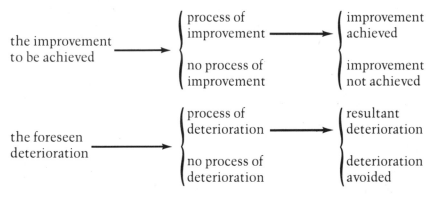

The various processes of improvement or deterioration, grouped in certain combinations, together constitute a *narrative cycle*. This is the term which Bremond uses to refer to such a structure. Each of the various processes has its own semantic contents. A number of possibilities have been further developed by Bremond. Applying a semantic label to an event makes it easier to compare the structures of different fabulas with one another. The following processes of improvement can be distinguished accordingly:

the fulfilment of the task
the intervention of allies
the elimination of the opponent
the negotiation
the attack
the satisfaction

These six possibilities – it is possible to conceive of other possibilities at the same level of abstraction – are not all necessary. When seen as the theoretical abstractions of concrete events, these possibilities can be found in many texts. Satisfaction, for example, can take the form of punishment, revenge, or reward, and these sorts of satisfaction can, in turn, be further specified.

The same applies to processes of deterioration. Bremond cites:

> the misstep
> the creation of an obligation
> the sacrifice
> the endured attack
> the endured punishment

A misstep can, for example, take the form of a mistake, an error, or a crime, and these variations can then assume other concrete forms. The initial situation in a fabula will always be a state of deficiency in which one or more actors want to introduce changes. The development of the fabula reveals that, according to certain patterns, the process of change involves an improvement or a deterioration with regard to the initial situation.

Other Principles of Structure

The events selected can be related to one another in a variety of ways. For this reason, one should not refer to *the* structure of a fabula, but to *a* structure. Bremond's model can be used as a basis, but it can also be left out of consideration, not because it would be invalid but because we can foresee that the results would not be very relevant to the fabula in question.

The following suggestions are not further elaborated. They are presented in order to give an idea of the multitude of possibilities, and, in so doing, to make clear that structures are formed by the investigating subject, on the basis of data, in this case on the basis of selected events combined with other data. These possibilities are intended to give some impression of the ways in which we can introduce structures into a collection of data. This does not imply that we can work at random. The structures must be built on the basis of data, the relationship between the data and what is done with it must be made explicit, and some degree of relevancy must be foreseen. Although the weather in Virginia Woolf's *To the Lighthouse* is often cold and raw, it does not seem relevant to contrast the events that occur in cold weather with those that occur in good or neutral weather conditions in order to establish a principle of structure.

More senseless still is to weight events during which actors stand against those during which they sit. Nevertheless, both categories could lead to a fairly relevant structure in some fabulas.

First, the events can be grouped on the basis of the *identity of the actors involved*. If the chronological order is maintained or reconstructed, the fabula is segmented into phrases. For example: actor A is the subject from event 1 through 6, actor B is the subject from event 7 through 15, etc. (see section 3, below, for the term 'subject'). The same can be done on the basis of the object, the actor who experiences the action. Further structuring is also possible. The events in which the two most important actors are confronted by one another can be contrasted with events in which only one of these two actors is involved with another, secondary, actor, etc.

Second, classification is possible on the basis of the *nature of the confrontation*. Is there verbal (spoken), mental (via thoughts, feelings, observations), or bodily contact? Are these contacts successful, do they fail, or is this impossible to determine? Such data can help to discover meanings in many difficult modern texts. If, for example, the contact between the two most important actors is predominantly mental and unsuccessful, we could conclude, if other data confirmed our conclusion, that the theme is alienation, a pre-eminently twentieth-century theme. The relationship between bodily and mental contact can suggest another theme.

Third, the events can be placed against *time lapse*. Some events can occur at the same time, others succeed one another. These latter form a linked series, sometimes 'interrupted' by a span of time in which nothing occurs, at least nothing that is narrated.

Fourth, the *locations* at which events occur can also lead to the formation of a structure. Depending upon the fabula in question, different oppositions can be relevant: inside-outside, above-below, city-country, here-there, etc. (Lotman 1973, 330).

These possibilities can be combined with one another. We can foresee, for example, that actor A is always the subject when the events occur inside, and actor B when the scene shifts to the outside; or that the contact always or almost always fails in one case while it succeeds in another; or that A especially desires verbal contact and B mental contact. An intuitive choice, necessitated by the simple fact that we cannot investigate everything, can be made explicit by means of our analysis. This carries with it the advantage of allowing us to pursue our own interests to a great extent while keeping to the same intersubjectively understandable model of analysis.

3   ACTORS

Selection

In defining the concept of 'event' we already used the term 'actors.' In the selection of events and the formation of sequences, actors always were important elements. In the following paragraphs, therefore, actors will be regarded in their relation to the sequences of events which – as follows from our definition – they cause or undergo. In order to begin to analyse this, it is necessary first to select which actors must be taken into consideration and which not. In some fabulas there are actors who have no functional part in the structures of that fabula because they do not cause or undergo *functional* events. Actors of this type may be left out of consideration. What has been said earlier also applies here: the initial disregard of an actor does not mean that this actor is without significance. It only means that this particular actor does not form part of the functional category, and therefore need not be taken into consideration. Well-known examples are the porters and maids who open the front doors in many nineteenth-century novels. Such actors act, they open the door, and thus they fit the definition of actors, but their action does not belong to the category of functional events. Therefore they fall outside the scope of this analysis. This is not to say that they may not be meaningful as an indication of a certain social stratification; and in that case they contribute to the representation of bourgeois society given in such a novel. They might also serve as an indication of a specific use of space; they guard the boundary between inside and outside. A comparison between actors of this type and, for instance, St Peter, the porter of the gate to heaven, might have interesting results. In order to acquire insight into the relations between events, it is necessary to limit the actors to the category of functional actors. Doing so one may rely on the earlier analysis of events. If this analysis has been skipped, an intuitive summary of the event may provide a preliminary starting point which might be tested later, for instance by drawing selective samples. This procedure, however, entails a vicious circle when one makes the summary with a certain subdivision of the actors already in mind. A middle-of-the-road solution might be to ask several people to write a summary, and to use the elements they have in common.

Classes of Actors

80

An important aspect of understanding the fabula is the subdivision of its actors into classes. Taking as a basis the presupposition that human thinking and action is directed towards an aim, one constructs a model which represents the relations to the aim. This model claims universal validity for its operative principle and is not limited to invented fabulas. In what follows, an analogy has been postulated between the structure of the fabula and that of the sentence. We must remember, however, that this homology is nothing but a practical point of departure: it is not carried out with full consistency and is based exclusively on analogies of a logical nature. It seems best, therefore, to regard the analogy between the structure of the fabula and that of the sentence as merely useful for didactic purposes. It allows one to illustrate the categories of the fabula in terms of the well-known structure of the sentence, with which most people have, to a certain extent, been familiar since their primary-school days.

As mentioned earlier, the model starts from a teleological relation between the elements of the story: the actors have an intention: they aspire towards an aim. That aspiration is the achievement of something agreeable or favourable, or the evasion of something disagreeable or unfavourable. The verbs *to wish* and *to fear* indicate this teleological relation and are, therefore, used as abstractions of the intentional connections between elements.

The classes of actors we call *actants*. An actant is a class of actors that shares a certain characteristic quality. That shared characteristic is related to the teleology of the fabula as a whole. An actant is therefore a class of actors whose members have an identical relation to the aspect of *telos* which constitutes the principle of the fabula. That relation we call the *function* (F).

Subject and Object

The first and most important relation is between the actor who follows an aim and that aim itself. That relation may be compared to that between subject and direct object in a sentence. The first two classes of actors to be distinguished, therefore, are *subject* and *object*: an actor X aspires towards goal Y. X is a subject-actant, Y an object-actant. For instance, in a typical love story the slots may be filled as follows: John – wants to marry – Mary. John is subject, Mary object, and the element of intention of the fabula takes the form of 'wanting to marry.'

The object is not always a person. The subject may also aspire towards reaching a certain state. In Stendhal's *The Red and the Black*, for instance, one might detect the following scheme: Julien – wants to acquire – power; or: Julien – aspires towards – becoming a powerful man. Other objects of intention found in fabulas are riches, possessions, wisdom, love, happiness, a place in heaven, a bed to die in, an increase in salary, a just society, etc. Thus the actant, and also its concrete embodiment the actor, are, in theory, disconnected from the embodiment in a person. This is implied in our structural approach. However, since, as was said earlier, the principle of the fabula resides in its aspect of intention, the practical result is that the subject is usually a person or a personified animal (in animal fables) or an object.

The following examples give an impression of the multiplicity of possibilities which can be 'translated' into this basic structural scheme:

	actor/actant-subject	function	actor/actant-object
a	John	wants to marry	Mary
b	Anna Wulf	wants to become	an independent woman
c	The old people	want to prevent	the discovery of their crime
d	Maigret	wants to know	the identity of the murderer
e	The killer	wants to avoid	Maigret's discovery
f	Marxists	want to bring about	a classless society
g	Tom Thumb	wants to have	a safe return
h	Scheherazade	wants to prevent	the king's killing her

The reader has undoubtedly recognized in this series a number of well-known fabulas and/or types of fabulas. They have been chosen from very different types of texts: an epistolary novel (a); a feminist novel (b); a nineteenth century novel (c); a modern detective novel (d and e); a work of social philosophy (f), a fairy tale (g), and a story sequence from folk literature (h). We shall return to these examples. At present we only need to realize that it is indeed likely that in very many if not all fabulas, a similar scheme can be pointed to.

Power and Receiver

The intention of the subject is in itself not sufficient to reach the
object. There are always powers who either allow it to reach its aim or
prevent it from doing so. This relation (F) might be seen as a form of
communication, and one may, consequently, distinguish a class of
actors – consisting of those who support the subject in the realization
of its intention, supply the object, or allow it to be supplied or given –
whom we shall call the *power*. The person to whom the object is given
is the *receiver*. The French terms used by Greimas are *destinateur* and
destinataire, and 'sender' and 'receiver' are their most literal translation.
It must be borne in mind, however, that 'sender' suggests an active
intervention or an active participation, and this does not always apply.

The power is in many cases not a person but an abstraction: e.g.
society, fate, time, human self-centredness, cleverness. The receiver
may also be embodied in a person. Thus a typology of fabulas might be
related to the concretization of this actant: in fairy tales the 'sender' is
mostly a person, often a king who under certain conditions gives his
daughter in marriage to the aspiring subject. In psychological novels, a
character trait of the subject itself is often the power which either facilitates or blocks the achievement of the aim. In many so-called 'realistic'
nineteenth-century novels the class structure of bourgeois society is
decisive – one is determined for life by one's social background. It is
also possible that several powers are in play at the same time. A combination of a character trait (ambition) and a social power (the division
into rich and poor) may conflict as positive and negative power.

The *receiver* is often the same person as the subject. S/he desires
something or somebody for him- or herself. But, since this is not always
the case, it is necessary to specify this class of actors.

In principle the subject and the power predominate more, or are more
active in a grammatical sense, than the object and the receiver, because
they are the agent, or the (grammatical) subject, either of the function
of intention/evasion or of giving/receiving.

We have already mentioned the possibility of the coalescence of two
actants into one actor or the reverse, the concretization of one actant,
the power, in several specific powers. This forces us to realize that the
basis of our model is the principle of *numerical inequality*; and that
this principle, however problematic it may seem, is at once the model's
justification. In principle all actants are represented in each fabula:

without actants no relations, without relations no process, without process no fabula. But the number of actors is unlimited. It may happen that in one fabula we find only one actor, a heroine who, for instance, is at war with herself, her passions, her madness and so on. On the other hand, it is also possible that large numbers of actors, whole crowds, armies, or university groups form together *one* actant. An example of the coalescence of four distinct actants into two actors is, again, the typical love story in which the receiver is the longing lover himself and the power coalesces with the object: she 'gives' herself.

He: subject + receiver
She: object + power

On the basis of this analysis one may gain insight into the relations between the powers that form the basis of such a fabula. Seen grammatically, the active subject is passive in his role of receiver: he must wait and see whether he will receive the desired object. On the other hand, the passive object is also subject, and therefore more autonomous in the role of power. The apparently passive object actant is, as power, the decisive factor in the background. The forces have been equally divided over the two actors. An inversion of roles would, therefore, not mean an inversion of power, and give no reason for the 'he' to panic.

The examples of the previous sections may now be expanded:

	subject	function	object
a	John	wants to marry	Mary
b	Anna Wulf	wants to become	an independent woman
c	The old people	want to prevent	the discovery of their crime
d	Maigret	wants to know	the identity of the murderer
e	The killer	wants to avoid	Maigret's discovery
f	Marxists	want to bring about	a classless society
g	Tom Thumb	wants to have	a safe return
h	Scheherazade	wants to prevent	the king's killing her

	power	function	receiver
a	Mary	is prepared to marry	John
b	the existing social structure	makes it impossible	for her(self)

c fate/time	make it impossible to hide their disgrace	from themselves and Ottilie
d his psychological insight	allows him to do so	to the benefit of himself, the police, and society
e his obsession and Maigret's insight	make it impossible	for the killer
f history	makes it impossible	for mankind
g his cleverness	brings that about	for himself and his brothers
h her powers of narrative	have that effect	to her own benefit

Helper and Opponent

The categories discussed hitherto are both directly geared to the object, which is object both of desire and of communication. Both relations are necessary for the development of a fabula. But a fabula based on merely these two relations would end very soon: the subject wants something, and either gets it or not. Usually the process is not so simple. The aim is difficult to achieve. The subject meets with resistance on the way and receives help. We may distinguish a third relation which determines the *circumstances* under which the enterprise is brought to an end.

By analogy with the structure of the sentence, these two actants might be regarded as adverbial adjuncts. They are not related to the object by means of 'a verb,' but relate through such things as prepositions, e.g. *owing to, notwithstanding*, to the function that connects subject with object.

These actants are in many respects different from the others. They are not in direct relation to the object, but to the function that connects subject with object. At first sight they do not appear necessary to the action. In practice, however, they are often rather numerous. They determine the various adventures of the subject, who must sometimes overcome great opposition before s/he can reach his or her goal. In this analysis problems tend to present themselves. It is often difficult to see the difference between sender and helper. The following points of difference may help to solve this difficulty.

power	*helper*
has power over the whole enterprise	can give only incidental aid
is often abstract	is mostly concrete
often remains in the background	often comes to the fore
usually only one	usually multiple

The same points of difference can be pointed to between a negative sender, a power who prevents the subject from reaching the object, and an opponent.

Another problem relates to the reader's sympathy or antipathy, since the relations between actants are not the same as those between actants and reader. The helper is not always the person who acts to bring about the ending desired by the reader. When the subject seems unsympathetic to the reader, the helper will, most likely, be so too; and the sympathy of the reader will go towards the opponent of the subject. If one confuses these two areas of relationship one may easily mistake the division of forces.

The examples of page 27 may now be expanded. I give only a sample of the many possibilities. In *a*, for instance, Mary's father might be an opponent if he opposed the marriage; John's good job, Mary's determination, and an interceding aunt could be helpers. In *b* several of Anna's friends, social prejudice, her employer might be opponents: her best friend tries to give help which is not sufficient to reach her aim. In *c* the several children, their curiosity, the memories of Harold are opponents; the doctor and those of the children who keep silent, helpers. In *d* and *e* helpers of one are the opponents of the other: witnesses, meetings, circumstances that help to bring the solution about, a button left on the scene of murder, the murderer's alcoholism, a talkative concierge, etc. In *f* the proletariat is helper and the bourgeoisie opponent. In *g* the giant's wife and boots are helpers; the nightfall, the birds who eat the crumbs, and the giant's powers of smell, which tell him that prey is near, are opponents. In *h* every story Scheherazade tells is a helper, and the unremitting suspicion and jealousy of her husband opponents.

From these examples the conclusion may be drawn that each helper forms a necessary but in itself insufficient condition to reach the aim. Opponents must be overcome one by one, but such an act of overcoming does not guarantee a favourable ending: any moment a new opponent may loom. It is the presence of helpers and opponents which makes a fabula suspenseful and readable.

Further Specification

This model is *structural*: it describes a structure – the relations between different kinds of phenomena – and not, primarily, the phenomena themselves. As we saw earlier, this model results in a numerical inequality of actors and actants. It is not surprising that one class of actors comprises more than one actor. The reverse, the fact that one actor stands for several classes, can only be understood if one disconnects the concept of 'actor' from that of 'person': this is the reason why the term 'person' is avoided when discussing actants.

We have already indicated some causes of the numerical inequality between actors and actants. The relationship between subject and object is very important. It can be aimed at the appropriation of someone, something, or, on the other hand, a quality in oneself. In the first case the object is a separate actor, in the second not. In the first case the relationship is *objective*, aimed at an external object, in the second case the relationship is *subjective*, aimed at (an aspect of) the subject itself. This may entail the further splitting or merging of actors and actants, but need not do so. The merging of the power with the object and the receiver with subject occurs with frequency. One also notes the merging of power with subject when a character trait of the subject is of overriding importance. Perhaps we may take it as a rule that the greater the fabula's orientation towards the actual outside world, the greater the number of actants; to the degree in which the fabula is subjective, oriented towards the subject, the number of actors decreases.

Doubling

A fabula may have different subjects who are in opposition: a subject and an anti-subject. An anti-subject is not an opponent. An opponent opposes the subject at certain moments of the pursuit of his or her aim. It is this incidental opposition which determines the structural position. An anti-subject pursues his or her own object, and this pursuit is, at a certain moment, at cross purposes with that of the first subject. When an actant has his or her own program, his or her own aims, and acts to achieve this aim, s/he is an autonomous subject. It is also possible that a fabula has a second subject that does not come into opposition with the program of the first subject, but is entirely independent from it, or s/he may, consciously or not, give incidental aid or opposition to the achievement of the first subject's aim. In that case there are moments in the fabula when the different lines touch or cross. (Using a different terminology, we would speak of the difference between the various episodes of one plot, and various sub-plots. The appearance of a separate subject always indicates the existence of a sub-fabula.) In Couperus' *Of Old People*, for instance, we might regard some of the children and grandchildren as autonomous subjects. In his struggle to become an artist, Lot needs self-analysis as a helper. This helper proves an opponent when Lot gains insight into the emotional predisposition of his heritage, and when his aims begin to conflict with those of the old people.

It is also possible that the power consists of two actants, a positive and a negative one. In naturalistic novels we often note the opposition of personal will-power to social structure or heredity. It is likely that an extensive analysis of a number of naturalistic novels might give us as characteristic result the opposition of two powers as a form of fabula intermediate between the subjective and objective, between the one oriented towards the individual and the one directed towards the outside world.

Competence

Aside from *oppositions* there are other principles to further specify actants. Keeping in mind that the process of the fabula can be seen as the execution of a program, we may posit that each execution presupposes the possibility of the subject to proceed to execution. This possibility of the subject to act, the *competence*, may be of different kinds, which leads to further specification.

Greimas subdivides competence into the *determination* or *will* of the subject to proceed to action, the *power* or *possibility*, and the *knowledge* or *skill* necessary to execute the aim. On this basis some critics have distinguished three different kinds of subjects. This distinction, however, is not entirely clear. After all, each subject has the will to execute his or her program; if not we do not have a fabula. It is possible, on the other hand, to distinguish that *phase* of the fabula in which the virtual subject begins to want the execution of the program; this phase might be seen as the introduction to the fabula. The distinction between power/possibility and knowledge/skill, however, is a workable principle of differentiation. The giants, witches, and wolves of the fairy tale are actants of the first category, Tom Thumb of the second one. It may have struck the reader that in the analysis of example *g*, the one of Tom Thumb, we have paid little attention to the giant. We have only mentioned his power of smell. It is evident, however, that the giant plays an important part in the fabula, more important than, for instance, his wife or Tom's brothers. Merely classifying him as an opponent would be insufficient as a definition. He has his own program. He wants to find children and eat them. He reaches that goal in part: he finds children and eats them because he has the power to do so, owing to his physical force and size. Still, he does not fully reach his goal: he eats the wrong children. His program is at cross purposes with that of Tom Thumb, who aims at a safe return home. The giant does not catch Tom Thumb and his brothers, because Tom Thumb possesses the second kind of competence, knowledge and skill in the form of cleverness.

It would appear that in this example the specification coincides with the opposition between good and evil powers. In fairy tales this is certainly often the case. It also seems to apply to the classic detective story. Nevertheless, there is an important difference, especially in this respect. The examples *d* and *e* show that Maigret and the murderer are in opposition. Maigret's competence is one of skill and knowledge. However, so is that of the murderer; and it is in this respect that the detective story differs from the fairy tale. What characterizes the detective story is that the murderer fails in his or her competence: s/he makes a mistake. The detective novel has lately undergone a development that shows the attempt to break through the opposition of good and evil, as for instance in the novels of the Swedish team of writers Sjöwall and Wahlöö. It is striking that, especially in those novels, the hitherto fixed division of competence should be broken. The detective often reaches his or her goal by accident or sometimes not at all, as in *The Closed Room*. The 'sender' then is not the detective's insight, but fate. In other instances the detective reaches the aim through the manipulation of power. If, owing to his or her social position, the culprit is forced into such a tight corner that s/he is ripe and ready to give him- or herself up to the detective, the latter only needs to dispose of the power to mobilize the police in order to reach his or her aim.

Truth Value

The final factor leading to further specification of actants is that of truth value. By truth value we mean the 'reality' of the actants *within* the actantial structure. This specification is of importance not only with regard to the subject, but also with regard to the helpers and opponents. Often they are only *in appearance* what they seem to be; in reality they prove the opposite. A traitor has the appearance of a helper, but reveals him- or herself in the course of the story as an opponent. In the reverse case there are secret helpers: actors who help the subject who believes s/he is dealing with an opponent, or an actor who seems to help the subject while the latter does not realize that this actor is not at all related to his or her own enterprise. According to this specification we may distinguish certain categories of actors: liars, master figures, false heroes, invisible fairies, but also truth-tellers, false clues, sudden moments of inspiration or misgivings which instigate the subject to take wrong decisions, seducers, etc. The several possibilities are outlined in the following scheme:

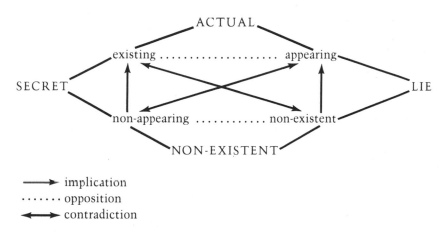

⟶ implication
······· opposition
⟵⟶ contradiction

This scheme shows the similarities and differences between the possible positions of actors with regard to 'truth.' 'Truth' exists in the coincidence of existence and appearance, of the identity and qualities of an actor on the one hand, and the impression s/he makes, his or her claims, on the other. When an actor *is* what s/he appears, s/he is true. When s/he does not put up an appearance, or, in other words hides who s/he is, this identity is secret. When s/he *neither is nor puts up an appearance*, s/he cannot exist as an actor; when s/he *appears* what s/he *is not*, this identity is a lie.

Not only actants but complete actantial schemes may be qualified as 'true' or 'false.' The frequent situation of the subject aspiring towards an illusory goal and finally realizing it might be accounted for in this way.

To this aspect of actantial analysis we might also try to relate a typology. Fabulas which show the predominating influence of a *secret* in their actantial structure (e.g. certain fairy tales and myths) might be opposed as a separate category to fabulas in which a *lie* determines structure. *Of Old People* hinges on the structural principle of the secret. So do detective stories. In spy novels the concept of the lie predominates. This division into classes of actors helps us to interpret, to set up typologies to sharpen our definitions of the literary movements, and to contrast fabulas that appear rather similar at first sight but prove different at vital points; on the other hand, it allows us to compare the actantial structures of apparently widely different fabulas. An analysis of this type *may* show unexpected aspects of meanings.

The supposition that the model we have outlined above is the only possible one would be absurd. Just as in the case of the analysis of events there are many other possibilities of approaching the matter which may or may not combine with our model. I briefly list a few below.

Other Divisions into Classes

In whatever way one regards literature, whether one values books as autonomous works of literary art, as products of an individual or group, as objects of communication, as a specific form of a sign system, one can never escape the obvious fact that literature is made by, for, and – usually – about people. Relations between people themselves and between people and the world will therefore almost always be of importance in fabulas. It is possible to describe in every fabula at least one type of relation between actors that is of a psychological or ideological nature, or of both simultaneously. Each of these relations may give a specific content to the relation between subject and power, between subject and anti-subject, but they may also be studied separately from the actantial model. On the basis of the information about the actors contained in the text, one may group them according to those principles which seem important in the frame of reference of the fabula or groups of fabulas under analysis.

First, *psychological relations* are of overriding importance in psychologically or psychoanalytically oriented criticism and determine the specification of actors into 'psychic instance.' It is often interesting to see how one actor relates to another as daughter to mother, as father to son, or son to mother, etc. Attempts have even been made to account for the difference between tragedy and comedy and their effect on the reader in this manner: in tragedy the son is guilty about the father, whom he, unconsciously, wants to replace; in comedy the father is guilty about the son and is consequently punished and replaced by the latter. In other cases the relationship between man and wife, or between child and adult, or between strong and weak personalities is of importance.

Second, *ideological relations* occur, next to psychological relationships, in many if not all fabulas. Whether it is the opposition between feudalism and liberalism, liberalism and socialism, patriarchy and egalitarianism, or more specific oppositions, actors must always deal with the ideological oppositions of the world in which they move. The opposition between the individual and the collective, or between the individual and the representatives of power, is often of importance both in medieval romances and in nineteenth-century realistic novels. In Kafka's novels this opposition is even of primary importance. Other oppositions of groups result in ideological relationships: black against white, men against women, employers against employees, 'haves' against 'have-nots', conformists against individualists, the 'normal' against the insane.

Third, *all kinds of different oppositions* may become important on the basis of data which, at first sight, do not have a psychological or ideological foundation, even if, on further consideration, it becomes apparent that they are often linked to psychological or ideological oppositions. On the basis of physical appearance groups may take shape; fair versus dark or red-haired, an opposition which in works of popular fiction seem to coincide with that between good and evil, thus conveying a racist ideology, or its parallel, the opposition of good-but-boring to exciting. Another ideologically coloured opposition often encountered in popular fiction is that between tall and slender on the one hand and short and fat on the other, which is related to its consequence: marriageability or inevitable spinsterhood. On the basis of past experience, heritage, possessions, relationships to third parties, age, and lifestyle, other groups may take shape which are often also related to psychological or ideological relationships. Moreover, in most cases a global analysis of the course of the fabula gives an indication of the direction in which to look.

4   TIME

Events have been defined as processes. A process is a change, a development, and presupposes therefore a *succession in time* or a *chronol-*

ogy. The events themselves happen during a certain period of time and they occur in a certain order. Both these aspects of the element time will be discussed here.

Duration: Two Kinds

The fabula of 'Tom Thumb' occupies a span of some three days. The first event, the overhearing of the parents' intention to rid themselves of their expensive children, takes place at night. So does the gathering of pebbles. The expedition to the wood and the return journey occupy the day following that night. The next night or, in some versions, a following night, at some indeterminate time, Tom Thumb again overhears his parents, again tries to collect pebbles, but finds himself prevented from leaving the house. The night after that the children get lost and wander into the giant's den. That night the giant eats his own children by mistake. The next day Tom Thumb and his brothers return home safely in possession of the seven-mile-boots, which guarantee a fixed income that will preclude the repetition of the fabula in the future. The time span of this fabula forms one continuous whole, possibly with the exception of the first night, which may be regarded as a prelude to the fabula proper. In three days the family's life changes substantially, from desperate poverty to happy prosperity. In 'Little Red Riding Hood' the whole fabula occupies only half a day. The principal narrative of the *Thousand and One Nights* presents a fabula which takes one season; that of *War and Peace* takes many years. The fabula of the Old Testament lasts many centuries. Maigret's investigations are, as a rule, finished in a few days, while Hercule Poirot and Miss Marple usually take longer. Classical tragedy even has rules about time. The time span of the fabula, which should not extend beyond one day and one night, thus functions as an aesthetic criterion or, at least, as a differential criterion with regard to genre. While 'unity of time' as a generic requirement remains restricted to classical tragedy, the time span of a fabula – which may show such wide differences – is also of significance in the fabulas of narrative texts. A first, global distinction might be that between *crisis* and *development*: the first term indicates a short span of time into which events have been compressed, the second a longer period of time which shows a development. In itself neither of these two forms has clear advantages over the other. It has sometimes been said that a development would be more realistic, more in accord with the experience of 'real life.' This seems doubtful, to say the least. In reality too, moments of crisis present themselves, moments during which, in a brief instant of time, the life of persons or an entire nation takes a decisive turn. It depends, moreover, on one's personal views about literature whether one prefers a greater degree of verisimilitude. It does seem likely, however, that a preference for one of these forms entails a certain vision of the fabula, and, often, of reality. It is likely, therefore, that such a form is meaningful in itself, or may be so.

Motivation of This Distinction

Certain types of fabulas are specifically appropriate for either of the two types of duration, or even dependent upon it. (Auto)biographies, *Bildungsromane*, war novels, frame narratives (*The Thousand and One Nights, Decameron*), and travel histories need a fairly long time span: the most important topic presented is precisely the passing of time. Other narrative texts, however, need a brief period of time, especially when describing a moment of crisis. Classical tragedy and the novels inspired by it are not the only examples. Many modern and contemporary novels and stories have also been written in the crisis form. The novels *La Modification* by Michel Butor and *Seize the Day* by Saul Bellow, each a well-known representative of new developments in the post-war novel, have, in this respect, been compared to classical tragedy. Though the fabula of Henry James' *The Ambassadors* does not cover a period of twenty-four hours but of several months, one may see it as a crisis nevertheless. Seen in the perspective of a lifetime, a few months is very little. It is difficult, therefore, to give fixed principles. However, this need not be an objection, because the distinction between crisis and development is relative. One form shades into the other. A fabula tends to a greater or lesser degree towards either one of the two forms, or covers the middle ground.

It is often also possible to distinguish both forms within one type of text. Sometimes, when this is the case, they may be considered characteristic of a certain sub-form, an author, a developmental phase of the type. Earlier we suggested a difference between the detective novels of Simenon and Agatha Christie. True, a more systematic analysis of their entire oeuvre would be needed to confirm the impression gained from a relatively small number of their novels. However, the point here is that in principle a distinction of this kind may result in a typology of texts. The preference for a crisis or development does not merely imply a certain vision of reality or a choice of a certain type of texts. Once selected, the two forms have implications for the construction of the fabula. I shall list a few here. The reader will discover other, and more specific, consequences.

1.a A development may present, in historical order, as much material as seems fit. It is not by accident that these novels are usually rather long.

1.b The selection of a crisis form implies a restriction: only brief periods from the life of the actor are presented.

2.a In a development, the global significance is built up slowly from the strings of events. The insights of the actors, and their mutual relationships, take shape through the quality of events.

2.b In a crisis, the significance is central and informs what we might call the surrounding elements. The crisis is representative, characteristic of the actors and their relationships.

3.a But a development too, requires selection. It is not an entire life-time which is presented, but parts from it; parts are skipped, abbreviated, summarized. Other parts are worked out, given an extra-detailed representation. From one novel to another we may find great differences in this representation of the development. This will be elaborated in chapter 2.

3.b The crisis, too, hardly ever occurs in its ideal form. Corneille met with the reproach that his *Cid* was too crowded with events for a twenty-four-hour span of time; the fight against the Moors, in addition to all the other events, could not possibly have taken place in so brief a time. In narrative – since it is, traditionally, less governed by precept than drama – the basic form is more easily varied and diverged from. In a crisis this does not happen primarily through summary, selection or highlighting – this will be covered in chapter 2, section 3 – but through asides. Thus we find recollections. In this manner the time span of *Of Old People* is extended from one season to sixty years; or we may encounter references to past and future: at the end of most fairy tales ('Tom Thumb' is no exception), the future of the protagonist(s) is briefly alluded to. There is another kind of diversion that may also serve to extend the time span of the crisis form: a minor actor may become the protagonist in his own fabula; in this way a sub-fabula is created.

These possibilities to extend the compass of the crisis and to com-

press the development are closely linked with the other aspect mentioned: that of chronology.

Chronology: Interruption and Parallelism

In the last subsection I pointed to the possibility of varying the time
sequence by means of elimination, or of condensation of duration, and
of the parallel development of several strands of the fabula. These
techniques have a bearing on the chronology of the fabula. Elimination
causes gaps in the sequence of chronology. A period of time is skipped,
often without being noticed by the reader. What has been eliminated?
This is, of course, a nonsensical question. The fabula is, after all,
nothing but the presentation of a series of events. No one is likely to
wonder what Tom Thumb's profession will be or at what age he started
to walk. Still, it often happens that omitted events are brought to the
fore in other parts of the text. Thus ellipsis – the omission of an element that belongs in a series – gains its power of signification. Robbe-
Grillet's *Voyeur* is, perhaps, the most spectacular illustration. In this
novel an event which, according to the further information given by
the fabula, must certainly have taken place is omitted. It would even
seem the most important event of the entire fabula: the sadistic murder
of a young girl, probably committed by the protagonist. Throughout
the fabula this actor, Mattias, exerts himself in filling this gap in time,
establishing an 'innocent' chronology. Until the very end it is not
clearly evident that Mattias is the murderer. Consequently, the fabula
cannot be fully described.

Though it is not as central as in *Le Voyeur*, in other narrative texts
ellipsis may also have a significant function. The sentence 'When they
left Tostes, Madame Bovary was pregnant,' which is so characteristic of
Flaubert's style, indicates by the ease with which it passes over the
event that the getting, and later having, of children is of very slight
importance to Emma Bovary, and the moment at which the child is
conceived is of none at all. Indeed, the sexual relationship between
Emma and Charles is, through the ellipsis of the event, fully 'represented.' In this case too, we are at no point in the fabula given full certainty about events.

The elaboration of parallel strings of one fabula makes it difficult to
recognize one single chronological sequence in that fabula. Several
events happen at the same time. It is not always possible to decide
whether the coincidence in time is partial or complete. The vagueness
of the chronology is, at times, just as significant as its painstaking

representation. In the Dutch novel *The Evenings*, by Gerard van het Reve, events happen exactly chronologically and this chronology is indicated with such accuracy that the suggestion arises of an obsession caused by a surplus of time. In Gabriel Garcia Marquez' *One Hundred Years of Solitude* the strict sequence of events is undercut from the inside, and readers who want to keep track of the course of the fabula find themselves powerless in face of the ever-multiplying story lines, which make one hundred years into an eternity. In so far as this effect is caused by changes, reversals in chronology, this problem belongs to the subject matter discussed in chapter 2, section 2. What concerns us here is that incomplete information, which is never filled out, leaves gaps in the constructed fabula, and thus blurs our impression of it. Also of importance here is the occurrence of parallelism, and the fact that *achronicity*, the impossibility of establishing a precise chronology, is often the result of the criss-crossing of several lines.

Logical Sequence

Sequence is a logical concept. It is a matter of logic to suppose that someone who arrives must have departed first; that old age follows youth, reconciliation quarrel, awakening sleep. On the basis of the information offered in the text, it is possible to find the chronology of the fabula even if the order is not sequential.

What is the advantage of doing so? Chronological sequences may be distinguished from other logical sequences. It is a frequent misconception that chronological and causal connections are always interrelated. It is true, of course, that one can only kill one's father after having been engendered. One may even do so because one is engendered by one's father; but there may also be entirely different reasons. Another ruling misconception is that what happens first is therefore better. For some people this has been a reason to proclaim the superiority of the male over the female, on the basis of the account of creation in Genesis 2; for others, on the basis of the same fragment, to denounce the account of creation as sexist. Both parties implicitly base their contention on the assumption that chronological priority entails a qualitative priority. The poetics of the Bible, however, does not at all allow such an interpretation. Falling back on purely chronological connections one may expose such preconceptions.

The time span may be contrasted and compared with chronology. A brief event, e.g. a meeting, succeeds a long-lasting event, e.g. a process of estrangement between two actors. In this order the meeting has or might have another significance and other consequences than it would have had had the order been inverted. Ordening the events in chronological sequence, one forms an impression of the difference between fabula and story. The interventions in chronology which become manifest may be significant for the vision of the fabula which they imply. We will discuss this in more detail in the next chapter.

5   LOCATION

Events happen somewhere. The locations where things happen may in principle be deduced. When we read

   a John was pushing his shopping cart when he suddenly saw his hated neighbour at the check-out counter

we may assume that the meeting place is the supermarket.

   b Elizabeth crossed the street

indicates a street, whether narrow or wide, long or short.

   c Sighing with pleasure he sank back into the pillows as she bent over him.

This sentence, also, leaves small doubt about the location of action.

When the location has not been indicated, readers will, in most cases, supply one. They will imagine the scene, and in order to do so, they have to situate it somewhere, however vague the imaginary place may be. The Russian critic Lotman has explained this by pointing at the predominance of the dimension of space in human imagination. In support of his contention he lists a number of convincing examples of spatial terms we use to indicate abstract concepts, such as 'infinite' for an 'immeasurably' large quantity, 'distance' for a deficient relationship between people. Incidentally, even the word 'relation' itself would seem to support Lotman's contention.

If spatial thinking is indeed a human property, it is not surprising that spatial elements play an important role in fabulas. It is, for instance, possible to make a note of the place of each fabula, and then to investigate whether a connection exists between the kind of events, the identity of the actors, and the location.

The subdivision of locations into groups is a manner of gaining insight into the relations between elements. A contrast between *inside* and *outside* is often relevant, where inside may carry the suggestion of protection, and outside that of danger. These meanings are not indissolubly tied to these oppositions; it is equally possible that *inside* suggests close confinement, and *outside* freedom, or that we see a combination of these meanings, or a development from one to the other. Thus in Colette's *Chéri*, Léa's bedroom is, at first, a safe haven for Chéri, but towards the end this place becomes a prison from which he escapes with barely concealed relief.

Another, related, opposition is the one between the centrally located square, which functions as the meeting place where actors are confronted with one another, and the surrounding world, where each actor has to fight for himself. City and country are contrasted in many romantic and realistic novels, sometimes as the sink of iniquity as opposed to idyllic innocence, or as a possibility to magically acquire riches in contrast to the labour of the farmers; or as the seat of power against the powerlessness of the country people.

This contrast too, may reverse itself when it appears that the riches of the city are also limited to a few and the common man in the slums is worse off than the farmer who can, at least, eat his own crops. In the British TV series *Upstairs Downstairs* the contrast between kitchen and drawing-room represents the radical difference between masters and servants. A public meeting-place such as a pub may function as neutral ground lending it a social function: it may be a meeting-place for companions in adversity who may gain courage from sympathy and solidarity; on the other hand, it may also be a place to take refuge in alcohol, leading to complete destruction, as in Zola's *Assommoir*.

Spatial oppositions may be much more abstract than the examples mentioned here. When several places, ordered in groups, can be related to psychological, ideological, and moral oppositions, location may function as an important principle of structure. For instance high-low, related to favourable-unfavourable, fortunate-unfortunate, is an opposition which Western literature has inherited from the late biblical vision of heaven and hell, and from Latin and Greek mythology. Far-near, open-closed, finite-infinite, together with familiar-strange, safe-unsafe, and accessible-inaccessible are oppositions often encountered.

Fabulas sometimes centre structurally on a spatial opposition. Thus Robinson Crusoe first flees the oppression of society by going to sea, then he is oppressed by his solitude, and finally he learns to convert his confinement into a form of freedom. Still, the longing for the society which oppressed him, but which also promised safety and protection from the adventure, continues; here we witness the crossing of another pair of opposites.

A special role may be played by the *boundary* between two opposed locations. Just as in Christian mythology purgatory mediates the opposition between heaven and hell, just so the front door may connote a crucial barrier for one intending to penetrate into certain circles. The shop as a transitory place between outside and inside, the sea between society and solitude, the beach between land and sea, gardens between city and country, all function as mediators. It is possible to be trapped in such places.

Many events are set in vehicles of transportation, such as trains, boats, carriages, airplanes. Consequently these events, e.g. murder in Agatha Christie, sex in Flaubert, meetings, quarrels, hold-ups, temporarily suspend the safe predictability and clarity of the social order.

6   REMARKS AND SOURCES

In this chapter I have outlined objects and processes as the most important elements of the fabula. First events were discussed, then actors. These two categories are considered the most relevant elements. In both cases I first discussed criteria for selection on the basis of which a large quantity of subject matter may be restricted on explicit grounds. Subsequently the relationship between the remaining elements was taken into consideration. Events were always seen in relation to the actors forming part of it, and the actors in relation to the events they initiate or suffer. With regard to events I paid special attention to different criteria of selection, while in discussing the actors I was primarily engaged in classification. This difference relates to the order in which both subjects were discussed; it is not necessary to discuss again the several criteria for selection when that has been done in the previous subsection, even if with regard to a different subject.

Finally, time and location have only been given summary attention. They will be discussed at greater length in the next chapter, for these elements are primarily interesting because of the way in which they are ordered and specified in the story.

The different subsections of this chapter show a clear resemblance. In every case I tried to describe the elements in their relationship to each other, and not as isolated units. One might call this approach structuralist: its assumption is that fixed relations between classes of phenomena form the basis of the narrative system of the fabula. I chose this approach because it offers, among other advantages, that of coherence. The different elements may thus be seen within the framework of one theoretical approach. Since every choice has its advantages as well as disadvantages, objections may be raised against this approach. The one mentioned most often is that it is reductive. This is inevitable: every choice is a limitation. That this approach is too strictly reductive in that it excludes other possible approaches is, however, not true.

A consequence of the approach taken in this book is that a great deal of attention was given to *classification*. When dealing with determined relationships between classes of phenomena, the ordering principles which form the basis of these classes must be made explicit. Classification, however, is for the literary scholar not a self-serving aim. Its use is instrumental: only when classification helps to provide greater insight into the phenomena constituting the classes is it meaningful in describing the text. Then significance may be derived from the fact that a phenomenon belongs to a certain class. The specific characteristics of one object may be described in the class to which they belong – or to which, against our expectation, they possibly do not belong.

Among other things, it is to emphasize that aspect of the approach that I have, in my examples, selected typological aspects just as often as specific texts. Classification *may* lead to the creation of typologies, even if the large quantity of inductive research necessary to set up and test a typology has hitherto been an obstacle to arrive at concrete results. Typologies, however, are often handled implicitly: when saying that a text shows 'such an original vision on society,' one implicitly assumes that a certain outlook on society forms the basis of the class of texts to which that particular one belongs.

Those who study comparative literature need typologies to structure their understanding of literary movements. Also the person analysing a single text may be helped with formal criteria to contrast a single text with a group of texts to which that one appears to belong entirely, or in part.

The criteria for the selection of events have been derived from Barthes (1966) and Hendricks (1973).

A critical application of Barthes' proposals has been made by Chatman (1969). The relations between events have been discussed according to the proposals of Bremond (1972). He distinguishes a third possibility for the combination of elementary series, juxtaposition. I have not included this possibility because to me it seems not of the same order as succession and embedding. 'Juxtaposition' does not result in a complete series of events, but in several visions of one and the same event. This issue is dealt with in chapter 2. The actantial model as it is presented here is derived from Greimas (1966). I disagree with his later proposal (e.g. 1976) to replace *opposant* and *adjuvant* with the concepts *anti-actant* and *co-actant*; the distinction between anti-subjects – autonomous subjects whose intentions are at cross purposes with those of the first subject – and incidental opponents would be lost. I would prefer to regard the duplication of the principal actant as a possibility, in addition to maintaining the original sixfold model. An alternative to Greimas' model is the less systematic but more inspiring sevenfold model of Souriau (1956). Of the structural models which have been designed, I have only referred to the best-known and most useful ones. All of them have, to a greater or lesser degree, been inspired by Propp, whose work only became widely known during the 1960s. The early work of Todorov and Van Dijk, some of Doležel's studies (e.g. 1973), and the work of Prince (1983) also belong to this development. Lotman's remarks on location are published in Lotman (1973).

2

Story: Aspects

1 PRELIMINARY REMARKS

I have called those features that distinguish the structured story from
the fabula the *aspects*. With this term I want to indicate that the story
– the middle of the three layers we distinguish in the narrative text –
does not consist of material different from that of the fabula, but that
this material is looked at from a certain, specific angle. If one regards
the fabula primarily as the product of *imagination*, the story could be
regarded as the result of an *ordering*. Obviously, this distinction is of a
theoretical nature only. In practice, different writers will proceed in
various manners. The aim of textual analysis is not to account for the
process of writing, but for the conditions of the process of reception.
How is it that a narrative text comes across to the reader in a certain
manner? Why do we find the same fabula beautiful when presented by
one writer and trite when presented by another? Why is it so difficult
in a simplified edition of a classic, or of a masterpiece of world literature, to preserve the effect of the original?

For one thing, this difference is probably the result of the working of
the text itself. Its effect changes with any alteration in the author's use
of language. But that is not the only reason. The effect will be at least
equally dependent on the way the material, the fabula, has been
handled. This is why many translations of texts – which necessarily
lose a substantial part of the original effect of the use of language, but
less of the technical aspects of the story – sometimes seem to relate

more closely to a first reader's reading experience than do adaptions, school editions, film versions and so on, which tend to interfere more seriously with the ordering of the material.

The best-known principle of ordering is the presentation of events in an order different from their chronological order. In the tradition of the theory of literature, this aspect has survived from the distinction between *fabula* and *suzjet* as used by the Russian formalists. We begin therefore again with the events. Characters – individualized actors – are now dealt with in the more traditional sense. From the remarks to Chapter 1 it will have become clear that I recommend an initial analysis of the relations between the various actors as abstract units, before proceeding to investigate individual features as looks, character, psychological qualities, and past. When those relations are clear, it is easier to distinguish between those relations and the relations between the reader and the characters, and the flows of sympathy and antipathy between the characters and from the reader to the individual characters. For the reader's view of characters and events will have to be accounted for with the aid of the concepts dealt with in this chapter. *Manipulation* originally meant simply 'handling,' 'treatment,' and even though its modern sense has shifted to include more unfavourable connotations, the original meaning is still synonymous to 'operation.' The fabula is 'treated,' and the reader is being manipulated by this treatment. It is basically at this level that ideology is inscribed. Such manipulation takes place not only in that actors are turned into specific characters, placed into specific spaces with mutual symbolic and circumstantial relations. The prime means of manipulation that has taken up an ever more important place in the literature of the last two centuries is what is traditionally known as *perspective*. The point of view from which the elements of the fabula are being presented is often of decisive importance for the meaning the reader will assign to the fabula. This concept plays a part in the most everyday situations. A conflict is best judged by letting each party give its own version of the events, its own *story*. Any treatment can be reduced to the *point of view* from which the image of the fabula and the (fictitious) world where it takes place are constructed. *Perspective*, then, is the technical aspect, the placing of the point of view in a specific agent.

If the first aspect that will be dealth with (deviations from chronology) is first and foremost a technical feature of the story – in most cases contributing only indirectly to the shaping of meaning – this chapter ends with an aspect (perspective) which has far more influence on meaning. The order in which the various aspects will be dealt with can also be explained in that sense: though all aspects point to narrative techniques, in most cases the importance of those various techniques for the shaping of meaning will become more significant as we go along.

2   SEQUENTIAL ORDERING

In these subsections, the relations are being explored which hold between the sequence of events in the story and their chronological order in the fabula. The latter order is a theoretical construction, which we can make on the basis of the laws of everyday logic which govern common reality. According to that logic one cannot arrive in a place before one has set out to go there. In a story that is possible, however.

> a John rang the neighbours' doorbell. He had so irresistibly felt the need to stand eye to eye with a human being that he had not been able to remain behind the sewing machine.

This is a quite ordinary passage, which no one would be surprised to come across in a narrative text. But anyone knows that in 'reality' (fictitious or not), the sequence of events must have been the other way round: *first* John must have felt the desire to go and see someone; *then* he acted accordingly and went to ring the doorbell.

Data are needed for such a confrontation between the ordering of events in the story and their sequence in the fabula. The latter will be deducible from explicit data or from indirect indications. In *a*, for example, the tenses of the verbs in the text indicate the sequence of events: simple past for the later event; past perfect for the preceding events. But even without such indications in the text there are data in the contents which we, with our sense of everyday logic, can combine in such a way that we can say, 'The ringing of that doorbell is likely to be the result of the occurrence of the desire.' It is not always possible to reconstruct the chronological sequence. In many experimental modern novels, we find, for instance, that matters are intentionally confused, the chronological relations expressly concealed. In such a case, obviously, we are powerless. But what is striking in these cases is that the chronological chaos we note is often still quite meaningful. This chaos can even be concealed behind apparent chronology, as in Márquez' *One Hundred Years of Solitude* and Duras' *L'Après-midi de Monsieur*

Andesmas. In other respects, these two novels are totally different. The significance, therefore, which can be attached to this astonishing game with chronology is equally different. The effect of Márquez' novel is to let people, generations, social contexts succeed each other in rapid turmoil in the course of a hundred years which seem to contain a history of mankind, to terminate in the absurd failure of (communal) life; Duras simply makes a man wait three hours for his daughter, and presents in those three hours the vision of a growing despair through a mixture of inertia and chronological chaos, indolence and the effort to endure that indolence – one of the tragical aspects of the ageing being, who has to continue living while, in fact, he is already dead. In neither novel is it easy to grasp the deviations in sequential ordering; both seem strictly chronological. Here too something that can be said of all branches of narratology applies: the failure of an analysis done with the aid of a systematic concept is a significant result in itself. On the other hand, it remains sometimes desirable that chronological relations be investigated when indications of chronological sequence can be found. At least one argument for the relevance of such an investigation – not always equally great – can be given.

As against various other art forms – architecture, visual arts – a written linguistic text is *linear*. One word follows another, one sentence follows another; and when one has finished the book, one has sometimes forgotten the beginning. In a narrative text, it is even possible to speak of a double linearity: that of the text, the series of sentences, and that of the fabula, the series of events. Moreover, narrative texts are usually fairly long, longer than most poems, which is why one usually reads them straight through, not retracing one's steps as one tends to do in the case of poems. There are various ways of breaking such strict linearity, forcing the reader to read more intensively. Deviations in sequential ordering may contribute to intenser reading; in the next chapter some other means will be discussed. If deviations in sequential ordering correspond with certain conventions, they will not stand out. They can, however, be so intricate as to exact the greatest exertions in following the story. In order not to lose the thread it is necessary to keep an eye on the sequential ordering, and the very effort forces one to reflect also on other elements and aspects. Playing with sequential ordering is not just a literary convention; it is also a means of drawing attention to certain things, to emphasize, to bring about aesthetic or psychological effects, to show various interpretations of an event, to indicate the subtle difference between expectation and realization, and much else besides. Turns of phrase such as

b Little could I then foresee

c Only yesterday I was thinking

point for instance at different interpretations of events. In *b* speaks perhaps a disillusioned old man looking back on the mistakes he made in his youth; in *c* someone may have recently discovered some important data on the grounds of which she has changed her opinion. These are mere guesses about fictitious examples that might be explained in different ways. Often, the misapprehensions of actors who are not in possession of the right information are 'afterwards' cleared up and explained in this way.

Differences between the arrangement in the story and the chronology of the fabula we call *chronological deviations* or *anachronies*. It goes without saying that no negative connotations should be attached to these terms; they are meant to be purely technical. There is no question of anything abnormal, but of something specific, something in which one text may differ from another. In nearly all novels anachrony can be found, even in *The Evenings* – despite the apparent chronological ordering. In most short stories, too, they can be found, albeit to a lesser extent. It seems to be the case that deviations from chronology tend to be more drastic when the fabula is more complex. This may be the result of the need to explain much in a complicated fabula. The explanation often takes the form of reference to the past. Also the difficulty of bringing the many different threads of a fabula together to form a coherent unity may create the need to refer back or point ahead. In particular, the 'classic' novel, after the model of the nineteenth-century realistic novel, makes much use of this possibility. A conventional construction of a novel is the beginning in *medias res*, which immerses the reader in the middle of the fabula. From this point s/he is referred back to the past, and from then on the story carries on more or less chronologically through to the end. Anachrony in itself, then, is by no means unusual.

In popular romances and other pulp fiction one encounters all kinds of variants of this form. However, anachrony *can* be used as a means for the realization of specific literary effects.

Direction: Possibilities

I shall discuss three aspects of chronological deviation successively: direction, distance, and range. For direction, there are two possibilities, Seen from that moment in the fabula which is being presented when the anachrony intervenes, the event presented in the anachrony lies either in the past or in the future. For the first category the term retroversion may be used; for the second, anticipation is a suitable term. I avoid the more common terms 'flashback' and 'flash-forward' because of their vagueness and psychological connotations. An example of a complete anachrony is to be found at the beginning of Homer's *Iliad*:

> d Sing, Goddess, the anger of Peleus' son Achilleus and its devastation, which put pains thousandfold upon the Achaians, hurled in their multitudes to the house of Hades strong souls of heroes, but gave their bodies to be the delicate feasting of dogs, of all birds, and the will of Zeus was accomplished since that time when first there stood in division of conflict Atreus' son the lord of men and brilliant Achilleus.
>
> What god was it then set them together in bitter collision? Zeus' son and Leto's, Apollo, who in anger at the king drove the foul pestilence along the host, and the people perished, since Atreus' son had dishonoured Chryses, priest of Apollo, when he came beside the fast ships of the Achaians to ransom back his daughter, carrying gifts beyond count and holding in his hands wound on a staff of gold the ribbons of Apollo who strikes from afar, and supplicated all the Achaians but above all Atreus' two sons, the marshals of the people: 'Sons of Atreus and you other strong-greaved Achaians, to you may the gods grant who have their homes on Olympos Priams' city to be plundered and a fair homecoming thereafter, but may you give me back my own daughter and take the ransom, giving honour to Zeus' son who strikes from afar, Apollo.'   (*The Iliad of Homer*, translated with an introduction by Richmond Lattimore [23rd edition; Chicago and London: University of Chicago Press, 1974], book one, p. 59)

The first object presented here is the grudge of Achilles. Subsequently we are told about the distress of the Achaeans, which resulted from it. Then the dispute between Achilles and Agamemnon is treated, which, as the direct cause of Achilles' anger, should precede it. The disease (the plague) is, in turn, the cause of the dispute, and the insult to Chryses was its cause in turn. We indicate the five units presented with A, B, C, D, E in the order in which they are presented in the story. Chronologically, their positions are 4, 5, 3, 2, 1, so that the anachronies can be represented by the formula A4-B5-C3-D2-E1: with the exception of the beginning, they form a direct return to the past. This complex beginning of the *Iliad* answers the convention which prescribes that one indicate what the story will be about. The apparently endless series of causes and effects indicates, moreover, how strongly the vicissitudes of human beings are determined by powers beyond them. And at the same time the reader is, already at the beginning, presented with a summary of the book's contents: that which the muse is asked to sing is what the reader will hear.

Another example, from a modern story this time, shows an entirely different sequential ordering:

> *e* A I saw that he could not take it. With a haggard face he looked at what was left of Massuro. He wanted a *reason* – otherwise, where was he? And the only thing that could pass for a reason, with a great deal of good (and occult) faith, was fear. B But there was no fear. Massuro hadn't known what fear was. C I knew Massuro well, in a manner of speaking. D So I shall tell it to you as if you were a friend, Gentlemen, although it's a mystery to me what you will do with the information when you have it.
>
> E Two years ago, when he was posted to my section at Potapègo, I happened to be standing jabbering to the village headman. The truck from Kaukenau arrived, and out of the cab stepped a swarthy, heavily built fellow with a big head, round eyes and thick lips. F Then, suddenly, I saw his name in the Major's letter before me again. G "Heintje Massuro!" (Harry Mulisch, 'What Happened to Sergeant Massuro?' *Hudson Review*, 14 [1961] 1)

The capital letters indicate the various chronological parts into which the fragment can be divided. Chronologically, all parts but one precede the story-time proper, the moment when the I-narrator, reporting the events, addresses the Dutch authorities, the War Department, with the words: 'It is a calm man who is writing this to you – a man with the calm that comes to the surface when hope has fled.'

It can be inferred that we are going to be presented with a mystery story which has ended unhappily. In A the speaker is in contact with a medical officer – rather an emotional sort of contact, as far as we can judge. No wonder, since there is between them the 'remains' of a human body, the body of Massuro, who has gradually turned into stone, in a mysterious manner. B treats the possible fears of Massuro, who has already died in A. So in the fabula, B precedes A. C covers a longer period, let us say from the renewed acquaintance between Massuro and the speaker, and the beginning of the sinister events, whether or not caused by the fears mentioned in B. In D we return to the story's present: the I is writing his report to the department. E recalls the moment at which the renewed acquaintance in New Guinea took place, and thus immediately precedes C, or rather E introduces the beginning of C. F lies even further back in the past: the speaker recalls the moment when, before the arrival of Massuro, he sees his name mentioned in a letter. Indicating the various parts with capital letters, and their chronological position with figures, the following formula ensues: A5-B4-C3-D6-E2-F1-G2. The fragment began with a haggard look and confusion, it ends in the placidity of a renewed meeting with the man: 'Heintje Massuro!', where the contrast between the familiarity of the Dutch boy's name and the exotic surname is striking. In view of the mysterious events which befell the man in question, this contrast, combined with the conflicting circumstances of the actors (a conflict which is already present in the name of the place, *Dutch* New Guinea), is by no means accidental. The chronological sequence of events, so clearly violated here, is broadly maintained from this passage onwards. But this confused beginning has already given us a picture of the confusion which underlies the fabula as a whole.

Difficulties

I have ignored one thing in this analysis. The chronological deviations are not all of the same order. F, for instance, takes place in the 'consciousness' of the first-person actor. In fact, the event is not the *seeing* of the name, but the *remembering* of the seeing. In that sense the fragment is not a chronological deviation, and it belongs to E ('Then'). In many texts, however, one finds this type of 'unreal' anachrony almost exclusively. The so-called 'stream-of-consciousness' literature, for instance, limits itself to the reproduction of the 'contents of consciousness,' and would, therefore, not be subject to the analysis of chronology at all. In order to solve this problem, and also in order to be able to indicate in other texts the difference between such 'false' anachronies and others – such as E in the above example – the addition of *subjective* and *objective* may be introduced. A subjective anachrony, then, is an anachrony which can only be regarded as such if the 'contents of consciousness' lie in the past or the future; not the past of being 'conscious,' the moment of thinking itself.

A similar problem occurs when a retroversion or anticipation is presented as direct discourse. Properly speaking, here too there is no question of a real anachrony. The moment of *speech* is simply part of the (chronological) story; only in the contents are past or future mentioned. Example *a*, for example, could continue as follows:

> f Sobbing, John sat on his neighbour's couch, pouring out his woes. 'I didn't know, when I married Mary five years ago, that she would sacrifice everything to her work, did I? That I would be no more to her than a cheap servant, always at hand to pour her a drink and fetch her an ashtray?'

The outburst itself chronologically follows the ringing of the doorbell in *a*. But the substance of John's lament has to do with the past, his marriage five years ago, as well as the entire period from his wedding to the present moment. This problem of *narrative levels* will be treated in the next chapter. For the moment, we need only note that the above constitutes a retroversion of the *second degree*, since speech takes place on the second level.

A third problem arises when we attempt to determine the position of the narrative units we have distinguished with respect to each other. Which time should we consider the *primary story-time*: that is, the time in relation to which the other units may be called flash-forwards or anticipations? Naturally, the answer to this question is extremely relative. In *e*, I labelled the time in which the speaker writes the letter *primary*. With respect to this primary time, all the events which actually constitute the contents of the fabula, the gradual fossilization of Sergeant Massuro, are retroversions. If the rest of the story were now to be presented chronologically, it would be pointless to note in each sentence that we are concerned with fabula-time 2, the period of renewed acquaintance until the death of Massuro. There are texts, moreover, in which the relationship between story and fabula is so complex that a thorough analysis would be useless. In such cases, a rough indication of the different time units can suffice, while interesting or complex fragments may be studied in detail. This is the method which Genette has used in his analysis of Proust's *A la recherche du temps perdu*, a novel which spans more than a thousand pages. The question which time may be judged primary is in itself not particularly significant; what may be of importance is to place various time units in relation to each other. In Mulisch's text, for instance, it is also possible to take 2, the time of renewed acquaintance, as our starting-point and consequently to view all references to periods 3 up to and including 6, the writing of the letter to the Ministry of War, as anticipation.

Finally, a fourth problem may present itself. It is possible that the anachronies may be embedded in each other, intertwined to such an extent that it becomes extremely difficult to analyse them. Such is the case already, in fact, with the second-degree retroversion in *f*: 'when I married her five years ago.' The contents of John's words are a retroversion: 'I didn't know ... did I?' belong to it, but that which follows, the substance of the *knowing* is, with respect to 'five years ago,' in its turn a (subjective) anticipation; a fact which is borne out clearly by the form of the verb itself, 'would sacrifice.'

These four problems can all be solved. I have raised them mainly to dispel the illusion that such a sequential analysis is simple, but also to indicate the myriad possibilities of variation available to us if we wish to create a story from a fabula.

One final problem, however, is in some cases insoluble. Once again example *e* may serve as an illustration. There I stated that C covers the period between the renewed acquaintance of the I-speaker with Massuro and the latter's death. That this is the period concerned seems probable in view of the fact that it is during this section of time that the events occurred which the speaker must relate. However, when we continue to read Mulisch's text, it becomes clear that the two actors also 'kind of' knew each other in the past. Consequently, it is no longer possible to determine whether C refers to the period in New Guinea alone, or whether the time that they knew each other in Holland is also included. To use a term derived from linguistics, we could here refer to *chronological homonymy*. In the same way that, in certain contexts, it is impossible to ascertain whether the word *bank* refers to a financial institution or the side of a river, so too in this case it is impossible to determine which period in the fabula is being referred to. And just as it is possible to use puns to achieve certain effects (confusion, humour, a sense of the absurd), so too chronological homonymy may be purposefully employed for the same reason. After all, in the case of Massuro, we have already been confronted with traces of confusion between the periods in Holland and New Guinea.

Distance: Kinds

By 'distance' we mean that an event presented in an anachrony is separated by an interval, large or small, from the 'present,' that is, from the moment in the development of the fabula with which the narrative is concerned at the time the anachrony interrupts it. For simplicity's sake, let us again return to example *e*. The arrival of Massuro in Potapègo occurs, as is indicated, *two years* prior to the writing of the letter. The other time-units are more difficult to pinpoint, although we do know that A should be placed after the death of Massuro and shortly before the writing of the letter, since the doctor's examination and the writing of the letter are both part of the administrative winding-up of the extraordinary decease, the certification of the cause of death, a process which is usually carried on with all possible speed. Somewhat later in the text we notice that this period covers six days.

In Butor's *La Modification* the distance is much greater. The primary story-time is the train journey from Paris to Rome. The subjective retro-versions to the past, and the broken marriage of the man making that journey, span a distance of years. Facts from the 'present,' things observed during the journey, are associated with facts stored in his memory. Clearly, all the flashbacks in this narrative are subjective.

On the basis of 'distance' we may distinguish two kinds of anachrony. Whenever a retroversion takes place completely outside the time span of the primary fabula, we refer to an *external analepsis*, an external retroversion. This is the case in *La Modification*, if we take only the return journey to be the primary fabula. If the retroversion occurs within the time span of the primary fabula, then we refer to an *internal analepsis*, an internal retroversion. If the retroversion begins outside the primary time span and ends within it, we refer to a *mixed retro-version*. Let us return to example *e*. Fragment A becomes an internal retroversion, if we take as our primary time span the period running from the renewed acquaintance until the 'present,' the writing of the letter. If, however, we view only the writing of the letter as the primary fabula, all retroversions become external.

It seems wisest to opt for that solution, which enables us to account for the greatest number of phenomena. Consequently, in this case, our

choice must fall on the first one. Thus, we establish as our primary
time span the period between the meeting and the writing. If we then,
as I proposed above, view fragment C as a chronological homonymy,
this retroversion becomes a mixed one: starting before the meeting in
Potapègo, it continues until the death of Massuro. Although I have
only given examples of retroversions, the same applies to anticipations
– though these occur much less frequently. With respect to the latter,
too, three possibilities may be discerned: external, internal, and mixed.

Functions

External retroversions often provide indications about the antecedents,
the past of the actors concerned, in so far as that past can be of importance for the interpretation of events. I have already stated that in *La
Modification* the subjective retroversions explained the man's disgust
with his wife and his nervousness about the confrontation with his
mistress. The very fact that these are subjective retroversions increases,
in this case, the explanatory function: disgust is subjective, after all. At
one point in 'What Happened to Sergeant Massuro' an anecdote is
recalled about the schooldays of the two actors, their first meeting, the
mutual feelings of friendship which neither of the two ever expressed.
This anecdote elucidates the odd, sober relationship between the two
men in New Guinea, which, in its turn, is an explanation of the narrator's inability to explain Massuro's strange death, while he so positively
denies that fear was the cause. All of this corresponds to the other facts
we have discovered in this text. Because of all these data the peculiar
atmosphere of menacing mystery in this text becomes more and more
obvious.
　　Internal retroversions may (partly) overlap with the primary narrative, they may 'overtake' it. They do not do so when the information
communicated by the internal retroversion is new, when it is a side-
track of the fabula. Such is the case when information is given about a
newly introduced actor, who has been concerned with other things
'during' the events of the primary fabula which afterwards turn out to
have been of importance.
　　If the contents of an internal retroversion overlap that of the primary
fabula, then the retroversion usually serves as compensation for a gap
in the story. This occurs because the information was not yet complete.
There may, for instance, be a gap in chronological succession. When we
are told, in one chapter of a novel, that the heroine is pregnant and, at

the beginning of the next chapter, we find ourselves in the baby's room, by now in use, the information about the delivery is missing. In Victorian novels such a gap in the flow of information, such an ellipsis, will, for 'decency's' sake, usually not have been filled, but in principle it would be possible to erase it by means of an internal retroversion.

In addition to this complementary function, internal retroversions may have yet another function. When they do not fill up an ellipsis or *paralipsis* – i.e. lack of information concerning a sidetrack – but instead elaborate on information already given, they seem to be a repetition. The repetition of a previously described event usually serves to change, or add to, the emphasis on the meaning of that event. The same event is presented as more, or less, pleasant, innocent, or important than we had previously believed it to be. It is thus both *identical* and *different*: the facts are the same, but their meaning has changed. The past receives a different significance. In Proust, such internal retroversions form a part of the famous and specifically Proustian interruption of the linearity in searching for, and recovering of, the elusive past. But in much simpler literature too, frequent use is made of possibilities such as these. Detective novels and all kinds of texts which are constructed around mysteries, masquerades, and puzzles adopt this technique as an important structural device.

Span

By the term 'span' we mean the stretch of time covered by an anachrony. Like its distance, the span of an anachrony may vary greatly. If a letter states:

   h Last year, I went to Indonesia for a month.

the span of the retroversion is a month, while its distance is a year. In Couperus' *Of Old People* all the allusions to the murder in the Indies are subjective (when the old people again call the scene to mind) or they are second-degree (when they talk about it) external retroversions with a distance of sixty years, and a span that varies from a quarter of an hour to one night to, at times, a few days.

With respect to the span of an anachrony, we can again define two different types. The anachrony may be *incomplete* or *complete*. A retroversion, for instance, is incomplete if after a (short) span a forward jump is made once again. Disconnected information is thus given about a section of the past, or, in the case of an anticipation, of the future. In *Of Old People* the retroversions concerning the murder are incomplete, as, for that matter, they are in every detective novel. Only when all the consequences of the murder – in *Of Old People* the anxiety which has remained with them – are discussed up until the 'present' is the retroversion complete. Only then has the entire development of the retroversion, from its starting-point to its conclusion, been presented. All the antecedents have thus been completely recalled. This occurs quite frequently, to take one example out of many, in the tradition of beginning *in medias res*, where the narrative begins in the middle of the fabula and the preceding events are then recalled in their totality. This is a special kind of anachrony: the distance and the span cover each other exactly; the retroversion ends where it began.

A familiar example of an incomplete anachrony is the retroversion in which the origin of Ulysses' scar is explained in the nineteenth book of the *Odyssey*. When Ulysses, still incognito, appears in his own house and the female servant who had nursed him when he was a baby washes his feet according to the custom of hospitality, she recognizes him by his scar. She begins to cry out for joy, but Ulysses stops her. At that moment, the story is interrupted by a lengthy explanation of the way in which the young Ulysses had come by the scar. After this extensive retroversion the chronological narrative is resumed; Ulysses is still trying to silence his servant. The *distance* of this retroversion is many years; the span is a few days; the infliction of the wound and its healing.

The span of an anachrony is often more difficult to determine accurately than the distance. But in general it is sufficient to indicate the difference between complete and incomplete anachrony. There is yet another way of classifying anachronies on the basis of their spans: that is, by distinguishing between *punctual* and *durative* anachronies. These terms have been borrowed from the linguistic distinction of time-aspects of verb tenses. *Punctual* corresponds to the *preterite* in English, the *passé simple* in French, and the *aorist* in Greek. *Durative* indicates that the action takes longer: in French the *imparfait* is used to indicate a durative aspect, in English it is expressed by the use of the progressive form. *Punctual* is used in this paragraph to indicate that only one instant from the past or the future is evoked, the moment that the wound was inflicted on Ulysses; *durative* means that a somewhat longer period is involved, the days of convalescence that followed. Often, a punctual anachrony recalls a brief but significant event; that significance then justifies the anachrony, despite its short span. Durative anachronies usually sketch a situation which may or may not be the result of an event, recalled in a punctual anachrony. Sometimes this distinction covers that between incomplete and complete anachronies, as is the case in example *f*. The presentation of the marriage between Mary and John is both punctual and incomplete. That which follows, the situation of John who, after the romantic honeymoon period, feels neglected by his ambitious wife, may be labelled both durative and complete. But durative and complete do not by any means always coincide. In *Of Old People* the memory of the murder is itself a (subjective) punctual retroversion; that of the period following it, the uneasiness and the feeling of guilt, the doctor's blackmail, is a (subjective) durative, but incomplete, retroversion. These possibilities can determine, to a very great extent, the author's narrative 'style' and may even give insight into his or her view of life. Frequent use of punctual anachrony sometimes makes for a businesslike style; systematic combinations of punctual and durative retroversions can create – or at least add to – the impression that the narrative is developing according to clear, causative laws: a certain event causes a situation to emerge which makes another event possible, and so on. If durative retroversions are dominant, then the reader quickly receives the impression that nothing particularly spectacular is happening. The narrative appears to be a succession of inevitable situations.

Anticipation

Everything we have discussed up till now concerning anachrony is, in principle, applicable both to retroversions and to anticipations. It is no coincidence, however, that almost all the examples used have been retroversion. To begin with, anticipations occur much less frequently. They are mostly restricted to a single (frequently covert) allusion to the outcome of the fabula – an outcome which one must know, in order to recognize (in retrospect) the anticipations for what they are. They may serve to generate tension or to express a fatalistic vision of life.

One more or less traditional form of anticipation is the summary at the beginning. The rest of the story gives the explanation of the outcome presented at the beginning. This type of anticipation can suggest a sense of fatalism, or predestination: nothing can be done, we can only watch the progression towards the final result, in the hope that next time we may recognize the writing on the wall. This type robs the narrative of tension, at least a certain kind of tension. The tension generated by the question 'how is it going to end?' disappears; after all, we already know how it is going to end. However, another kind of tension may take its place, prompting questions like 'how could it have happened like this?', with such variants as 'how could the hero(ine) have been so stupid?' or 'how could society allow such a thing to happen?' or 'how did the hero(ine) find out about this?' and so on, according to the direction in which the conventions of the genre steer the reader. But so-called 'first-person' texts are most suitable for references to the future. A narrative which is related by a narrator who claims to be presenting his own past can easily contain allusions to the future, which, in relation to the story-time is 'the present' or may even already be the past. A sentence like

> i Little could I then suspect that ten years later I would again run into the man who is now my husband.

contains such an anticipation. In relation to the time of the fabula ('then') this sentence is an anticipation ('ten years later'), but in relation to the story-time ('now') it is a retroversion, although the distance of the retroversion is smaller than that of the retroversion in which (in the form of an anticipation) it has been embedded. Here again, it is a matter of how the investigator wishes to view the situation. Whether such a sentence is regarded as an anticipation or as a retroversion is of little importance; what is of importance is both the fact that there are three distinct moments involved, and the question of how they are related to each other.

Anticipations, too, can be grouped as internal or external, even though it is not always possible to establish the dividing line with absolute certainty. In *La Modification* Cecile's visit to Paris is constantly being evoked. By the end of the story we still do not know whether that visit will ever take place. That uncertainty fits in well with the overall defence of the man who is running away from the situation and does not really want to know it. The allusions to Cecile's moving house, all subjective anticipations, cannot be classified as internal or external, although it is probable that they are internal. Internal anticipations frequently complement a future ellipsis or paralipsis: things are made clear now, so that later on they can be skipped, or only mentioned in passing. Conversely, such anticipations may have a connecting or an accentuating function when they constitute nothing more than the marker 'I shall be coming back to this.' Such is the case in this book, for instance, whenever I am forced to touch briefly upon a subject that I would much rather discuss in detail later.

A highly effective use of anticipation is the so-called *iterative antici-pation*. In an iterative anticipation an event is presented as the first in a series. Such an anticipation often begins in the following way:

> j Then Reagan appeared on the screen, a spectacle that would
>   weigh on our spirits every Friday from now on.

Subsequently, the spectacle in question is presented in full detail and the reader is to view each particularity as an example of something that will occur again and again in the future. The fuller such a report, the less credible its iterative character. It is, after all, improbable that the same actions could be performed in exactly the same way every week, right down to the smallest detail. In such a case, one is apt to forget quickly that the event was the first of a series, and with its itera-tive character its anticipatory aspect dissolves. One obvious technical advantage of this form is that it offers a good opportunity for showing the scene through the eyes of an inquisitive newcomer, which makes its detailed character immediately more credible. Precisely this combi-nation of iterativeness and the uniqueness of the *first time* gives this form its special possibilities. Proust makes a characteristic use of this figure.

The novel we have already mentioned several times, Duras' *L'Après-midi de Monsieur Andesmas*, is constructed for the most part around the tension between the promise, made just before the beginning of the fabula presented, and the fulfilment of that promise, just after the end of the fabula. Both the anticipation of the promised return of Monsieur Andesmas' daughter and the uncertainty concerning the *distance* of that anticipation determine the importance of the events in the story, which ultimately consist of various phases of waiting.

Usually a distinction is made between those anticipations of which the realization is certain and those of which it is not. This distinction undergoes adaptation, however, when the terms *announcement* and *hint* are employed. Announcements are *explicit*. Mention is made of the fact that we are now concerned with something that will only take place later on. Adverbs such as 'later' and verbs such as 'expect' or 'promise' are used in the text or may be logically added to it. Hints are *implicit*. A hint is simply a germ, of which the germinating force can only be seen later. The clues in a detective novel often function as hints. In such cases, care must be taken to keep the knowledge from the reader, to prevent the understanding that these hints are anticipations; if not, the puzzle will be solved prematurely. On the other hand, it must remain possible for the attentive reader to glimpse their anticipatory nature.

It is this possibility that initiates the game between story and reader; *announcements* work against the tension; hints increase it, because the trained readers of detective fiction will be asking themselves constantly whether a certain detail is an anticipation or not. This curiosity can then be manipulated by means of *false* hints: details that create the suggestion of being clues, but turn out in the end to have been only details after all. A good example of the above is offered in Hawthorne's *The Blithedale Romance*. There, the impulses are often not really false, but turn out to be irrelevant.

Achrony

In the preceding paragraphs we have assumed that it is possible to determine, with more or less precision, the direction, the distance, and the span of a deviation in chronology. This, however, is not always the case. Sometimes, although we may see clearly that we are dealing with a deviation, it will be impossible to define, either because the information cannot be sorted out, or because there is too little of it. We call such a deviation an *achrony*, a deviation of time which cannot be analysed any further.

Various kinds of deviations resembling achrony are possible. One of them has already been discussed briefly in connection with the problems involved in determining direction (see *Difficulties*, p. 56). That was the form anticipation-within-retroversion, referring forward within a back-reference. This form need not always lead to achrony. Example *f* seems clearly definable as an anticipation from within a retroversion and together forms a complex and complete second-degree retroversion. However, when an anticipation from within a retroversion brings us back once again into the 'present,' it can become difficult to continue to talk about a certain direction. If a continuation of *f* were to read:

   k When she asked me to marry her, she promised she would be
       home every evening, that she would have a lot of time for me.

a future which would have to be the 'present' is being evoked from within the past. This expected 'present' stands in shrill contrast to the realized 'present': instead of running home after work, Mary rings up more and more often to say that urgent business will keep her a few more hours ... The situation which is predicted in *k* should, as far as the passing of time is concerned, have been realized by now. Only reality has turned out differently, as if to give the lie to overconfidence in anticipations. Such an anticipation-within-retroversion, which verges on achrony, can have the effect of a confrontation between an expected and a realized 'present.'

A second possibility is the opposite form, the retroversion-within-anticipation. This occurs, for instance, when we are told beforehand how circumstances in the 'present' will be presented to us. The meaning of an event can only be made known later; and the coming of that revelation is announced 'now':

   l Later, John would understand that he had wrongly interpreted Mary's absence.

The revelation of John's mistake will come later, but 'now' it is being foreshadowed. At the moment of revelation reference is made to a mistake made in the past; but in relation to the future, that past is the 'present' evoked by means of a retroversion-within-anticipation.

A third possible anachrony, which comes close to achrony, may occur when an anticipation in relation to the fabula turns out to be a retroversion in the story. An event which has yet to take place chronologically has already been presented, e.g. in embedded speech, in the story. Then an allusion is made to it which is an anticipation with respect to the fabula, but a retroversion with respect to the story (Later John understood that ...).

In addition to these three types, which are difficult to define accurately because of their complex structure and, consequently, come close to achronies, there are two more possibilities of definite 'achrony'; that is, deviations which are impossible to analyse because of lack of information. To begin with, an achrony may be 'undated,' may not indicate anything about its direction, distance, or span. One example:

   m I have never seen him without his wig.

Here a relationship of sorts with the past is given. In a pinch, this sentence could be seen as a complete retroversion of indeterminate distance. In fact, however, nothing indicates whether the span is restricted to the past or not; in any case, it includes the 'present' if nothing establishes that the situation comes to an end. A second possibility lies in the grouping of events on the grounds of other than chronological criteria, without any mention of chronological sequence. Proust sometimes presents a whole series of events, all of which have occurred in the same place. Spatial connections thus replace chronological ones. If such a series were to be constructed solely according to spatial or any other criteria (association, for instance), the text would no longer fit the definition of narrative given in the introduction. But if such a series occurs in a narrative, in which chronological connections are indicated everywhere else, we are dealing, in any case, with an achrony. With this last form of achrony we have exhausted the possibilities for structuring the chronological flow within a story into a specific sequence. Here, the linearity of the fabula and the linearity of its presentation to the reader no longer have any correspondence at all.

3   RHYTHM

Background and Problems

Investigations into the relationship between the amount of time covered by the events of a fabula and the amount of time involved in presenting those events are already old. In the 1920s Percy Lubbock wrote his *Craft of Fiction,* in which he made a distinction between a *summarizing,* accelerating presentation and a broad, *scenic* one. Twenty years later in Germany, Günther Müller wrote a number of extensive studies on this subject. Students applied Müller's principles to a large number of texts.

   One fundamental problem of such research is the question of what to take as a measure of the speed of presentation, the rhythm. Usually, it is possible to calculate, at least approximately, the time covered by the events. Yet the problem is with what kind of time this time of the fabula should be compared. Is it the time taken up by the writing of the narrative, as has been proposed? Usually, not only is it impossible to discover what period of time was involved in writing but also this time is of little importance for the effect of the text on the reader. Should we take as a standard of measurement the time it takes to read the narrative? This varies. If necessary, a rough average reading-time per novel could be calculated. This reading-time would then, in principle, be comparable to the time covered by the performance of a play or music, even though this performance time does not vary with each receiver (listener or spectator) but with each performance. The end-product of these calculations remains dubious, since we are working with averages; and then relevance has still to be established, to say nothing of the problems involved in working them out. For the moment, we must conclude that the so-called *time of telling* (this is the term Müller and his followers employ) is not available to us, and that, therefore, the comparison between two times is impossible.

It is possible, however, to calculate the speed with which the various events are presented. Just as speed in traffic is gauged by juxtaposing the amount of time involved with the distance covered (s/he is doing sixty: s/he is travelling sixty kilometres in one hour), so too the amount of time covered by the fabula can be juxtaposed with the amount of space in the text each event requires: the number of pages, lines, or words. This is the solution Müller and his followers have chosen.

Quite a few objections have been raised to the analyses of the Günther Müller school, which sometimes extended these analyses very far indeed. Such investigations *can* lead to sterile line-counting, without any relevance to the interpretation of the text in question. That objection applies not only to this subject, however. Every research project must go on proving its own relevance over and over again; and it goes without saying that there is no point in initiating a detailed calculation of temporal relationships unless some degree of relevance can be predicted.

As I have said, then, such research should not simply be aimed at precise calculation of the number of words or lines per event; the amount of text set aside for each event only indicates something about how the *attention* is patterned. The attention paid to the various elements gives us a picture of the vision on the fabula, which is being communicated to the reader. That is why I have chosen to discuss this subject here and not in chapter 3. The attention paid to each element can only be analysed *in relation* to the attention paid to all the other elements. If we treat this division of attention as the main object of the investigation, we must not limit ourselves to counting lines only, but should aim at establishing comparisons, calculations as an aid. In fact, this was Müller's main aim too: the fact that some of his students have, at times, lost sight of that original goal does not diminish the interest of their enterprise.

Global Rhythm

In order to achieve an analysis of narrative rhythm it is necessary first to draw up a general survey of the course of time of the fabula. This point has already been discussed in the subsection *Chronology*. Once a survey has been drawn up of the amount of time covered by the various events or series of events, *episodes*, it becomes possible to use these data to determine the global rhythm. Let us take as an example a complete life-story of the kind frequently written in the nineteenth century. The fabula contains the birth of the hero, his childhood, adolescence, military service, first love, the period of social ambition, decline, and death. It is possible to determine the number of pages devoted to each episode. Often, this simple exercise alone will make clear that certain episodes are given more attention than others. Childhood, for instance, is often summarized quickly, while 'first love' is dwelt upon in much more detail. On the other hand, the novel may also reflect an even division of attention. In Dickens' *Dombey and Son*, for instance, the story begins with the birth of Paul Dombey. At that time, his father is forty-eight years old. After approximately one third of the story Paul dies, at about the age of twelve. The story continues on until Dombey's old age, so that we could say that, as far as rhythm is concerned, Paul's death takes place 'at the right moment,' for Dombey then has twenty-odd more years to live.

Whether or not the attention is spread more or less evenly across the fabula, there will always be an alternation of sorts between extensive and summarizing presentation. This alternation is generally viewed as the most important characteristic of the narrative genre; be that as it may, it is clearly an important marker. Lubbock already made a distinction between these two forms, the *scene* and the *summary*. It has been noted, and rightly so, that this relative contrast should be pushed through to its limit. On the one hand, we can distinguish the *ellipsis*, an omission in the story of a section of the fabula. When a certain part of the time covered by the fabula is given absolutely no attention at all, the amount of TF (time of the fabula) is infinitely much larger than the TS (story-time). On the other hand, we can distinguish the *pause*, when an element that takes no fabula-time (so an object, not a process) is presented in detail. TF is then infinitely smaller than TS. Usually, this is the case in descriptive or argumentative fragments. This will be discussed in the following chapter.

Both summary and slow-down should be viewed relatively, in relation to each other. The easiest way to set up such a comparison is to establish a kind of ideal tempo, a zero-line. Real *isochrony*, a complete coincidence of TF and TS, cannot be determined precisely. We may, however, assume that, for instance, a dialogue without commentary takes as long in TF as it does in TS. The dialogue, and in principle every *scene*, every detailed presentation of an event with a claim to isochrony, thus functions as a point of comparison. By *scene* we here mean a segment of text in which TF = TS. In total, five different tempi would thus become distinguishable:

$$
\begin{array}{lll}
\text{ellipsis} & \text{TF} = n \quad \text{TS} = 0 \quad \text{thus} & \text{TF} > \infty\, \text{TS} \\
\text{summary} & & \text{TF} > \text{TS} \\
\text{scene} & & \text{TF} \simeq \text{TS} \\
\text{slow-down} & & \text{TF} < \text{TS} \\
\text{pause} & \text{TF} = 0 \quad \text{TS} = n \quad \text{thus} & \text{TF} < \infty\, \text{TS}
\end{array}
$$

Here $>$ means longer than
   $<$ means shorter than
   ∞ means infinite
   $\simeq$ means is $\pm$ equal

My presupposition is that every narrative can be divided up into pieces, which each correspond to one of these five tempi. In the following paragraphs, I shall discuss a number of characteristics inherent to each tempo.

Ellipsis

A real ellipsis cannot be perceived. According to the definition, after all, nothing is indicated in the story about the amount of fabula-time involved. If nothing is indicated, we cannot know what should have been indicated either. All we can do, sometimes, is logically deduce on the basis of certain information that something has been omitted. That which has been omitted – the contents of the ellipsis – need not be unimportant; on the contrary, the event about which nothing is said may have been so painful that it is precisely for that reason it is being elided. Or the event is so difficult to put into words that it is preferable to maintain complete silence about it. Another possibility, which I have already mentioned, is the situation in which, though the event has taken place, the actor wants to deny that fact. By keeping silent about it, he attempts to undo it. Thus the ellipsis is used for magical purposes, as an exorcism.
   How are we to discover these ellipses, which can, apparently, be so important that it seems worth the trouble to look for them? To begin

with, our attention is sometimes directed towards an elided event because of a retroversion. It is not always possible to locate such an ellipsis exactly in the fabula. We know that something must have happened, and sometimes we know approximately where, but usually it is difficult to indicate the exact location.

It does sometimes occur, however, that an ellipsis is indicated. Mention is made of the time that has been skipped. If a text reads:

> *a* When I was back in New York after two years.

we know exactly how much time has been left out. It is even clearer when an ellipsis is mentioned in a separate sentence:

> *b* Two years passed.

In fact, this is no longer a real ellipsis, but could be called a minimal summary, or rather, a summary with maximum speed: two years in one sentence.

Such a pseudo-ellipsis, or mini-summary, can be expanded with a brief specification concerning its contents:

> *c* Two years of bitter poverty passed.

The pseudo-ellipsis is beginning to look more and more like a summary. Whether we still regard the next sentence as a pseudo-ellipsis or whether we now label it a summary simply depends on how far we wish to go: the borderline between these two tempi is flexible.

> *d* Two years of bitter poverty passed, in which she lost two children, became unemployed, and was evicted from her home because she could not pay the rent.

Summary

This last example was intended to show how difficult it is to set up an absolute dividing line; in fact, it is fairly clear that we should refer to it as a summary. In example *c* the content-specification indicated a *situation*. None of the events of those two elided years are mentioned, even though it is improbable that no events took place at all. In *d*, however, various events are presented, at least three, but probably four or more.

The children probably died one after the other and that loss then counts as two events. The unpaid rent implies a good many events, the landlord's visits, the woman's desperation and its expression, her attempts to find money and the failure of those attempts. The woman is evicted. What then? At that moment in the fabula, the situation changes. Consequently, the rhythm of the narrative changes. A slower tempo is adopted, the next event – a meeting? an inheritance? a discovery? – must alter the situation radically. Consequently, this key event receives all the attention. This, at least, is the pattern, in very general terms, in the tradition of the novel. The so-called 'dramatic climaxes' – events which have a strong influence on the course of the fabula – the turning-points, moments at which a situation changes, a line is broken, such events are presented extensively in scenes, while insignificant events – insignificant in the sense that they do not greatly influence the course of the fabula – are quickly summarized. The opening of Dickens' *Oliver Twist*, an outstanding example of a realistic novel, exhibits something like this rhythm. Oliver's birth is presented extensively: three pages. Then, at the age of nine months, the hero is sent to a charitable institution. The situation there is sketched in a page and a half, and suddenly Oliver is nine and is taken away: three pages. The rhythm of Flaubert's *Madame Bovary* is very different. Many events, which one could expect to have been presented as dramatic climaxes, are summarized rapidly, whereas routine events – for instance, situations that recur every week – are presented extensively. This reversal of the traditional rhythm is naturally very well suited to a fabula that reflects boredom, the emptiness of a person's existence. To a very great degree, the originality of Flaubert's work is determined by this technique. As should be clear from the above, the summary is a suitable instrument for presenting background information, or for connecting various scenes. The place of the summary in a story depends strongly on the type of fabula involved: a crisis-fabula will require much less summarizing than a developing fabula (see *Duration: two kinds*, p. 38).

Scene

If one comes to think of it the scene is, per definition, in the majority. That is unavoidable. The point is not, as I have already said, simply to count pages and gauge the significance of an event by means of figures. Such an investigation would only yield clues about the internal relations between the various tempi. This relation is not always the same.

Although traditionally an even alternation between summary and scene used to be the aim, in order neither to overtire the readers with too rapid a tempo nor to bore them with one that was too slow, in the course of time a development has made itself felt towards rejection of that stereotypical pattern. We have already seen that in *Madame Bovary* the scenes frequently present an event in extenso as an *example* of a whole series of such events. Every Thursday the heroine went to Rouen to visit her lover: thus a long scene follows, in which such a visit is presented in detail. The effect of this technique is to dull the newness of the event, to indicate that daily routine has once again re-established itself in Emma's life, at exactly that moment which was intended to demonstrate her efforts to break out of that routine. A hopeless enterprise, we therefore conclude. Proust, too, who was greatly inspired by Flaubert, showed a preference for scenes. But in his work they function somewhat differently. In *A la recherche du temps perdu* scenes are often the *first* of a series of similar scenes. This transforms them into anticipations. The curiosity, the intensity of the sensations of a 'first time' justify, in these instances, the lavishness of the presentation.

In a *scene* the duration of the fabula and that of the story are roughly the same. It is useful to indicate why such coincidence cannot be qualified with any other adverb than 'roughly.' Most scenes are full of retroversions, anticipations, non-narrative fragments such as general observations, or atemporal sections such as descriptions. This is under-standable once we realize that a truly synchronic scene, in which the duration of the fabula coincides completely with that of the presentation in the story, would be unreadable. The dead moments in a conversation, the nonsensical or unfinished remarks, are usually omitted. Even a writer who is trying to give precisely these aspects of a conversation their due – like Marguerite Duras – is forced to abridge them considerably, on pain of unreadability. If a writer wishes to fill out a scene, s/he will automatically employ more exciting material – material which can also serve to connect the preceding and the following chapters. Thus, a scene is often a central moment, from which the narrative can proceed in any direction. In such cases, the scene is actually anti-linear. The coincidence of TF and TS is then no more than appearance. A very clear example of this paradox is *L'Etranger* by Camus. This novel, in which chronological sequence is maintained, consists almost entirely of scenes. Naturally, these scenes cannot possibly coincide completely with the time of the fabula. After all, the latter covers a few days. In fact, they are pseudo-scenes, scenes which are presented in a strongly accelerated manner, and in which a myriad of invisible ellipses must be present. This lack of synchrony is even explicitly indicated, as Meursault, the protagonist, regularly consults his watch to ascertain that it is, again, much later. The same thing happens in *The Evenings*. The scenes, usually slow paced, are used in these novels to indicate the rapidity of time together with the immeasurable emptiness in spending it: an excess of time is reflected by giving the suggestion of too little time. The scene is the most appropriate form to do so.

Slow-down

We need only be brief on the subject of the slow-down, a tempo that stands in direct contrast to the summary. In practice this tempo occurs very seldom. It is already extremely difficult to achieve perfect synchrony in a scene, because the presentation is soon experienced as too slow. Still, the theoretical possibility of this tempo cannot be ignored. Although it is, in general, set aside for use in small sections of the narrative only, it can nevertheless have an extremely evocative effect. At moments of great suspense, slow-down may work like a magnifying glass. This is the case, for instance, in *L'Après-midi de Monsieur Andesmas*, where at the end a few seconds of the fabula span pages. The occasion is the long-awaited arrival of Monsieur Andesmas' daughter. The girl's voice, her footsteps, can all be heard, and still it takes a terribly long time before she actually appears. This last event we are not even allowed to see. As if to indicate that her late arrival is unalterably too late for her father, as proof that he has lost her, the arrival itself is not presented at all. Consequently, it occurs outside the story and, strictly speaking, outside the fabula. The fabula of the novel spans the time just after her departure to the time just before her return.

Sometimes, a brief slowing down may occur within a scene, in these cases often reinforced, by, for instance, a subjective retroversion. The most frequent instance is the arrival of a visitor or a letter. In the short time between the ringing of the bell and the opening of the door, the actor is bombarded by all sorts of thoughts, his nerves are taut – a whole life passes through his mind and it takes pages before he actually opens the door.

Pause

Pauses occur much more frequently. This term includes all narrative sections in which no movement of the fabula-time is implied. A great deal of attention is paid to one element, and in the meantime the fabula remains stationary. When it is again continued later on, no time has passed. In that case, we are dealing with a pause. It goes without saying that a pause has a strongly retarding effect; on the other hand, the reader easily forgets that the fabula has been stopped, whereas in a slow-down our attention is directed towards the fact that the passage of time has slowed down.

In various periods of literary history, different opinions have been held about pauses. In Homer, pauses are avoided. Often descriptions of objects are replaced by retroversions, which also have a slowing down effect, but still replace the broken line of time by another temporal sequence.

This is the case during the explanation of Ulysses' scar, by which his old nurse recognizes him on his return. The shield of Achilles is described in a retroversion, while it is being made. Agamemnon's armour is described while he is putting it on, so that we can here no longer refer to an interruption, but to a scene.

During the period of naturalism, the pause was less of a problem. After all, the goal of these novels was usually to sketch a picture of reality. In order to do that a good many object-descriptions were necessary, while the flow of the fabula-time was of secondary importance. Lengthy descriptive sections and generalized, argumentative expositions are certainly not exceptions in the novels of this period. The pause was an accepted tempo. And when such descriptions led to excessively long interruptions of the fabula, their presence was justified by tying them to the vision of an onlooker. This last solution was adopted systematically by the post-naturalistic novelists. Whenever a long description had to be inserted, they made sure that the seam was hidden. In Zola's novels, this takes the following form. An actor *looks* at an object, and what s/he sees is described. The passing of a certain amount of time is thus implied, so that such descriptions do not constitute a real pause, but a scene. That flow of time is indicated by means of a verb of perception – usually *to see* – supported, in many cases, by adverbs of time: *firstly, subsequently, and then finally* all suggest the passing of time, even if everything else indicates that there can hardly be any question of passing time. The pause is thus concealed.

The complex question of the delimitation and definition of descriptive and argumentative sections as opposed to narrative sections will be discussed briefly in the following chapter. Here it is only important to note that such sections disrupt the flow of time and function, therefore, as pauses.

4 FREQUENCY

The two aspects of time treated above, order and rhythm, are often distorted by a third aspect, which has, in the development of literary theory, as yet received little attention. Genette labels this aspect *frequency*. By this he means the numerical relationship between the events in the fabula and those in the story.

The phenomenon of *repetition*, which is under discussion here, has always had a dubious side. Two events are never exactly the same. The first event of a series differs from the one that follows it, if only because it is the first and the other is not. Strictly speaking, the same goes for verbal repetition in a text: only one can be the first. Yet a series such as

  a I went to bed early. I turned in betimes. I was in bed before dark.

will be seen as a repetition of one and the same event: the actor went to bed early. Obviously, it is the onlooker, in this case the investigator, who remembers the similarities between the events of a series and ignores the differences. When I here refer to a repetition, I mean different events or alternative presentations of events, which show similarities; these similarities are then our main focus of attention. The most recurrent frequency is the singular presentation of a singular event.

  b She came at length and opened the door to her sister's importunities.   ('The Story of an Hour' from Kate Chopin's *Portraits*)

However, a story entirely constructed of such singular presentations would create a highly peculiar and ragged effect. Usually, a combination of this and other possible frequencies is employed. A second possibility is that an event occurs more often and is presented as often as it occurs. Thus, there is a repetition on both levels so that, again, we should really term this a singular presentation. This is not the case if the event occurs often and is presented often, but not as often as it occurs. If something happens every day in the course of three months, and it is presented five times, numerical disproportion results. Whether such a frequency creates a strongly repetitive effect or not depends on the nature of the event and the amount of attention paid to it. 'The more banal the event, the less striking the repetition' could serve as a rough guideline.

iteration

We refer to a real *repetition* when an event occurs only once and is presented a number of times. Some experimental novels employ this possibility lavishly: in general, it is used with much more discretion. Moreover, the repetition may be disguised to a certain extent by stylistic variations, as in example *a*. Sometimes variations in 'perspective' are also used to justify the need for a repetition: the event may be the same, but each actor views it in his or her own way. This device was used regularly in the eighteenth-century epistolary novel. Another famous example is Faulkner's *The Sound and the Fury*. Every internal retroversion or anticipation that does not fill in an ellipsis belongs to this frequency. After all, these constitute repetitions of something that has already been mentioned before.

The reverse of a repetition is an *iterative presentation*: a whole series of identical events is presented at once. We have already seen examples of this. Flaubert and Proust make systematic use of iteration. Iterative presentation used to be regarded as subordinate to singular presentation. It was employed to sketch a background, against which the singular events were highlighted. Flaubert was the first to give iteration a dominating position in his work. Proust went even further: his novel consists for the most part of iterative scenes. These are often so extensive that their iterative nature becomes questionable. One visit is described in eighty pages: the conversations, the gestures, the guests, everything is presented in detail. It is no longer credible that such a visit is an example of weekly visits, performed year in year out. This then is a case of pseudo-iteration.

There are three types of iteration. If they are *generalizing* and are concerned with general facts that also exist outside the fabula, then they come very close to situation-descriptions. The above-mentioned opening of *Oliver Twist* is a good example: the scene in the poorhouse is an instance of what it was like, in general, in the poorhouses of that time, apart from the fabula of this poor little boy. One may also highlight events which are related to a specific fabula but which exceed its time span. These we could call *external* iterations.

    c And yet she had loved him, sometimes.   ('The Story of an Hour')

This love has sometimes, though not often, been felt, but is mentioned only once. The period intended lies outside the borders of the fabula, and the iteration could therefore be termed external. It is not generalizing, however, as it concerns this one woman, the woman who is the actor in the fabula. In addition, we also find 'normal' iteration. In order to favour a quick, efficient notation I have drawn up a formula, according to which these frequency-types may be defined; let me add emphatically, that this formula has no pretensions to greater precision.

    1 F/1S: singular: one event, one presentation
    nF/nS: plurisingular: various events, various presentations
    nF/mS: varisingular: various events, various presentations,
    unequal in number
    1F/nS: repetitive: one event, various presentations
    nF/1S: iterative: various events, one presentation

    In the preceding sections we have discussed the temporal organization of the events of a story. Just as in the preceding section, this organization pertains to the structural effect of the events – seen as *processes* – in the majority of narrative texts. In the following sections aspects will be discussed which pertain to *objects*: actors and places.

5   FROM ACTORS TO CHARACTERS

Up to now, I have constantly used the term *actor*. I did so because I wished to include the various acting entities in the broadest possible term. The term covers a larger area than a more specific term could do. In other words, a dog, a machine, could act as an actor. In this section, I shall employ the term *character*. By this, I mean the actor provided with distinctive characteristics which together create the effect of a character. In the course of this section, the difference between the general, abstract term *actor* and the more specific term *character* will gradually become clearer. To begin with, let it suffice to say that a character resembles a human being and an actor need not necessarily do so. What that resemblance means in narratological terms, and what its limitations are, will be discussed later. For the moment, let us assume that a character is an actor with distinctive human characteristics. In this view, an *actor* is a structural position, while a *character* is a complex semantic unit.

26

The term *actant* indicates a *class* of actors, viewed in relation to each other. These mutual relations are determined by each actant's relation to the events. This approach to the actant does not take the actor's semantic function as a specific narrative unit into account. On the level of the story, characters differ from each other. In that sense they are individual. On the basis of the characteristics they have been allotted, they each function in a different way with respect to the reader. The latter gets to know them, more or less than other characters, finds them more or less appealing, identifies more or less easily with them. The aim of these paragraphs is not to *determine* (define) the characters (*who* are they?), but to *characterize* them (*what* are they and how do we find out?).

Problems

3 6

Characters resemble people. Literature is written by, for, and about people. That remains a truism, so banal that we often tend to forget it, and so problematic that we as often repress it with the same ease. On the other hand, the people with whom literature is concerned are not real people. They are imitation, fantasy, fabricated creatures: paper people, without flesh and blood. That no one has yet succeeded in constructing a complete and coherent theory of character is probably precisely because of this human aspect. The character is not a human being, but it resembles one. It has no real psyche, personality, ideology, or competence to act, but it does possess characteristics which make psychological and ideological description possible.

The first problem that arises when we attempt to account for the character-effect is that of drawing a clear dividing line between the human person and the character. The resemblance between the two is too great for that: we even go so far as to identify with the character, to cry, to laugh, and to search for or with it. We can attempt to solve this first problem by restricting our investigation to only those facts that are presented to us in the form of discourse. But this is only an initial delimitation, which is difficult to make more specific and which, in any case, does not solve all our problems. Within the material of the story – the entire mass of information presented to us by the narrating agent – borderlines are also difficult to draw. When we come across a detailed portrait of a character that has already been mentioned, we are justified in saying that that information – that portrait – 'belongs to' the character, it 'creates' the character, maps it out, builds it up. But everyone knows that a story contains other information which, though connected less directly with a certain character, contributes as much to the image of that character that is offered to the reader. It is not always easy, or even possible, to determine which material should be included in the description of a character.

Another problem is the division of characters into the kinds of categories literary criticism is so fond of. The classical distinction between *round* and *flat characters*, which has been employed for more than half a century, was based on psychological criteria. *Round characters* are like 'complex' persons, who undergo a change in the course of the story, and remain capable of surprising the reader. *Flat characters* are stable, stereotypical characters that exhibit/contain nothing surprising. Even if such classifications were to be moulded into manageable distinctions (attempts to do so do not encourage optimism), they would still only be applicable to a limited corpus: that of the psychological narrative. Entire genres, such as fairy tales, detective fiction, and pulp fiction, thus remain excluded from observation because all their characters are 'flat.' A distinction is possible on the basis of the actantial model, but only one that is concerned with the relations between the elements of the fabula, and not with the way in which these are 'fleshed out' in the story. Again, this would not enable us to define the specific vision on each character which the reader receives. We need to establish a criterion for the classification of specific narrative characters, if we are to explain the character-effect. A summary of the kind of information the readers have at their disposal in order to construct an image of a character, and one of the information they actually use while doing so, should make this possible.

The so-called extra-textual situation creates yet another problem: the influence of reality on the story, in so far as reality plays a part in it. Even if we do not wish to study the relations between text and context as a separate object of research, we cannot ignore the fact that direct or indirect knowledge of the context of certain characters contributes significantly to their meaning. The character President Eisenhower in Coover's *The Public Burning* is not the factual president of the United States, Eisenhower as we know him from historical evidence. But the impression we receive of that character depends, to a very great extent, on the confrontation between our own image of Eisenhower and the image that the story offers, which in its turn is determined by another context. The influence of data from reality is all the more difficult to determine since the personal situation, knowledge, background, historical moment, and so on of the reader are here involved.

Finally, the description of a character is always strongly coloured by the ideology of the investigators, who are usually unaware of their own ideological principles. Consequently, what is presented as a description is an implicit value-judgment. Characters are attacked or defended as if they were people. Moreover, author and character are viewed as one and the same. Existentialist criticism tended to do this. Emotions flared at the publication of Nabokov's *Lolita*. Humbert's mentality was all wrong; the man was an immoral hypocrite, and quotations from the text could prove this. If, however, we examine all the utterances of the first-person speaker, then, to say the least, a much more problematic picture emerges. And even if the first-person speaker is an immoral hypocrite, this does not then mean that the entire novel is immoral, or was ever meant to be. A good deal more research would be necessary to back up the claim of immorality, always limited to the context in which the particular morality is generally accepted.

These problems have not been raised for nothing. They should neither be denied nor ignored. Rather, they should be clearly formulated and categorized. Ideological discussions and value-judgments should not be censured, but should be classified correctly. Only then can they be discussed, and this can only benefit the analysis. The model below may help to make this procedure easier.

Predictability

On the basis of certain data the character becomes more or less predictable. These data determine him or her. To begin with, the data concern information that relates to the non-textual situation, in so far as the reader is acquainted with it. We shall treat that section of reality to which the information about the person refers as a frame of reference. The latter is never entirely the same for each reader, or for reader and writer. By frame of reference we here mean information that may with some certainty be called communal. For every American reader, Coover's Eisenhower fits into a frame of reference.

Historical characters are often brought to life in novels. Napoleon we even meet quite regularly. Legendary characters, like King Arthur or Santa Claus, also fit into a frame of reference. In contrast to what one might expect at first, historical characters are not more strongly determined than legendary ones. On the contrary, legendary characters are expected to exhibit a certain stereotypical behaviour and set attributes; if the story were to depart too far from these set characteristics, they would no longer be recognizable. Santa Claus loves children;

his whole status as a legendary character is based on that. It seems difficult to imagine a story about Santa Claus in which the good man plays a dirty trick on a child; such stories, however, can and do exist.

Where historical characters are concerned the possibilities are somewhat greater. Because we are more certain of the identity of such a character, an unfamiliar side can be shown and will be accepted more easily: a tyrant during a fit of weakness; a saint in doubt or in temptation; a party-going revolutionary. But here too the possibilities are limited because of the frame of reference. A mature Napoleon presented as a poor wretch would create a very odd effect: he would no longer be Napoleon. In yet another way, mythic and allegorical characters fit a pattern of expectation, established in the basis of our frame of reference. The goddess of Justice cannot make unfair decisions without destroying her identity as a character. Only for those who know that this character is usually blind will a wide-eyed goddess of Justice be a problem. All these characters, which we could label *referential* characters because of their obvious slots in a frame of reference, act according to the pattern that we are familiar with from other sources. Or not. In both cases, the image we receive of them is determined to a large extent by the confrontation between, on the one hand, our previous knowledge and the expectations it creates, and on the other, the realization of the character in the narrative. Opting for a referential character implies, in this respect, opting for such confrontation. The ensuing determination, and the extent to which it is realized, may therefore be an interesting object for research.

Referential characters are more strongly determined than other characters. But, in fact, every character is more or less predictable, from the very first time it is presented onwards. Every mention of the identity of the character contains information that limits other possibilities. Reference to a character by means of a personal pronoun alone limits its gender. And, in general, this then sets off a whole series of limitations. A *he* cannot find himself unintentionally pregnant. A *she* cannot, in general, become either a Catholic priest or a rapist. These limitations are also related to the actantial position which the character holds (see chapter 1, section 3). In so far as they are traditionally determined, these limitations are subject to change. Closer analysis will probably reveal that in much traditional literature, women can only function as subject in certain fabulas, in which the object is a characteristic of the subject (happiness, wisdom) and not a concrete object that would necessitate a long journey or a physically taxing

ordeal. Thus, the topics treated in chapter 1, section 3 and the specifi-
cations of the characters discussed here are very closely and mutuallly
related. When a character is indicated with *I* these sexual restrictions
do not (yet) apply, but in that case other restrictions are possible. The
character, the I, is not presented from a spatial distance, which, in turn,
involves all sorts of other limitations. When the character is allotted
its own name, this determines not only its sex/gender (as a rule) but
also its social status, geographical origin, sometimes even more. Names
can also be *motivated*, can have a bearing upon some of the character's
characteristics. To this category belong not only names such as Tom
Thumb and Snow White. Agatha Christie's Poirot has a pear-shaped
head. Miss Marple is not only a woman, but is also unmarried, and that
state implies a number of stereotypical qualities conventionally connected with elderly unmarried ladies: inquisitiveness, a great deal of
spare time, reliability, innocence, naïvety, qualities that are necessary
for the development of the fabulas. In fact, because of the inseparable
link between the title Miss and the name Marple – reason also to consider the 'Miss' a proper name – this character is also highly referential.

   A portrait, the description of the exterior character, further limits the
possibilities even more. If a character is old, it does different things
than if it were young. If it is attractive, it lives differently from the
way it would live if it were unattractive. Profession, too, greatly determines the frame in which the events take place or from which they
receive their meaning. A thatcher falls from a roof (*L'Assommoir*, Zola);
sooner or later a miner will be trapped in a shaft that has collapsed
(*Germinal, Sans Famille*) if he doesn't die of some kind of lung disease; a
soldier dies at the front or is sent to faraway countries (Hemingway, *A
Farewell to Arms*). None of these determining factors is absolutely certain. The fact that profession, sex, external factors, or quirks of personality are mentioned creates an expectation. The story may fulfil it, but
may just as easily frustrate it.

   Genre plays a part in a character's predictability. A detective must, in
principle, find the murderer. This genre-bound expectation is sometimes broken; for instance, in *The Locked Room* by Sjöwall and
Wahlöo, where the character is arrested for another crime and the
mysteries are never entirely solved. The alterations which a genre is
subject to are influenced by the interplay between the evocation, satisfaction, and frustration of expectations. The stronger the determination, the greater the shift away from tension generated by questions
concerning the outcome and towards the tension generated by the

question whether the character will realize its own determination and/or break away from it. A character's predictability is closely related to the character's frame of reference. But the effect of this predictability also depends on the reader's atttitude with respect to literature and the book he or she is reading. Is s/he strongly inclined to 'fill in' or will s/he let him- or herself be led by the story? Does s/he read quickly or does s/he interrupt the reading often to stop and think about it? Information about a character's predictability can only provide clues to its potential determination; real predictability has not been proven. It is interesting to analyse the way in which possible determination emerges in the story. In many ways, we *afterwards* conclude that a certain detail about a character was related to an event, or to a whole series of events. Establishing connections, coherence, in this way, is not the same as signalling predictability *beforehand*. Predictability makes it easy to find coherence, it contributes to the formation of one image of one character out of an abundance of information. But it is not the only way in which that image can be formed. We can distinguish various relations between data, on the basis of which an image of a character can also be formed.

Construction of Contents

When a character appears for the first time, we do not yet know very much about it. The qualities that are implied in that first presentation are not all 'grasped' by the reader. In the course of the narrative the relevant characteristics are repeated so often – in a different form, however – that they emerge more and more clearly. Repetition is thus an important principle of the construction of the image of a character. Only when our attention has been focused on it a few times do we begin to regard, for instance, Frits van Egters' tendency (in *The Evenings*) to notice baldness in others as a characteristic of this character. And only then do we realize that this characteristic recurs constantly throughout the rest of the narrative.

In addition to repetition, the piling up of data also fulfils a function in the construction of an image. The *accumulation* of characteristics causes odd facts to coalesce, complement each other, and then form a whole: the image of a character. In *The Evenings* we notice not only Frits' preoccupation with baldness, but his obsession with other signs of decay as well, autumn, illness, old age, death, time. And these facts *together* convey a clear picture of the character, in the areas where unconnected data might have been striking, but would not have been particularly meaningful.

3

In the third place, *relations* with others also determine the image of a character. The character's relation to itself in an earlier phase also belongs to this category. These relations can be divided into *similarities* and *contrasts*. We need a semantic model to describe these categories, and one will be presented in the next subsection.

4

Finally, characters may change. The changes or transformations which a character undergoes sometimes alter the entire configuration of character as it looked during the analysis of mutual relations. Once a character's most important characteristics have been selected, it is easier to trace transformations and to describe them clearly.

Repetition, accumulation, relations to other characters, and transformations are four different principles which work together to construct the image of a character. Their effect can only be described, however, when the contents of the outline of the character have been roughly filled in.

Filling In the Outline

How do we determine which are a character's relevant characteristics and which are of secondary importance? One method is the selection of relevant *semantic axes*. Semantic axes are pairs of contrary meanings. Characteristics like *large* and *small* could be a relevant semantic axis; or *rich-poor*, or *man-woman, kind-unkind, reactionary-progressive*. The *selection* of the relevant semantic axes involves focusing, out of all the characteristics mentioned – usually an unmanageably large number – only on those axes that determine the image of the largest possible number of characters, positively or negatively. Of the axes which involve only a few or even one character, only those are analysed which are 'strong' (striking or exceptional) or which are related to an important event. Such a selection involves the ideological position of the analyst and also points at ideological stands represented in the story, and can therefore be a powerful tool for critique. Once a selection has been made of the relevant semantic axes, it can function as a means of mapping out the similarities and oppositions between the persons. With the help of this information we can determine the qualifications with which a character is endowed. Some qualifications belong to a social or a family role. In that case, determination comes into play. A character is, for instance, a farmer and a father. Both roles strongly determine what qualifications he receives. In a case like this, no one will be surprised if the character – in a traditional story – is strong, hard-working, and strict. The opposite of strong is weak; of hard-working, lazy; of strict, flexible. The other pole of these axes is probably filled by a character with an equally clear role. It will hardly surprise anyone if the farmer is contrasted with his weak, effeminate student-son. In accordance with prejudice, the young man will be lazy. The qualification 'flexible' is hardly applicable to the son; he does not occupy the kind of position of power that allows him the choice between strictness and leniency. This pole will be filled – how could it be otherwise? – by his mother. Should we now attempt to collect the various qualifications we have isolated for all these characters, we would end up with a diagram of the following kind, which for the sake of clarity, has been sketchily outlined.

character qualification / role	strength	diligence	flexibility
farmer/father	+	+	–
student/son	–	–	ϕ
mother	ϕ	ϕ	+

Here + = positive pole
      – = negative pole
      ϕ = unmarked

This results in a picture of a set of characters, strongly determined by social and family roles. The father is not only qualified as strong; he is also the most strongly qualified character. Two of the three qualifications mark him as positive; all three apply to him. The mother plays a less prominent part in accordance with her social position. She is marked by one quality alone, though a positive one. The young man is marked twice, both times negatively. The mutual relations between the characters are immediately visible. In this way, more complexly structured sets of characters may also be mapped out.

Once we analyse which characters are marked by a certain semantic axis, we can set up, by using such a diagram as this, a hierarchy of strongly and weakly marked characters. If a number of characters are marked by the same axes with the same values (positive or negative), they can be regarded as *synonymous* characters: characters with the same content. Inconspicuous duplications of characters can thus be exposed. One need not, however, restrict oneself to a sometimes overly simplistic two-way division of axes. It can be useful to determine whether differences of *degree* and *modality* are evident within each qualification. *Degree* can transform a polar scale into a sliding scale: very strong, reasonably strong, not strong enough, somewhat weak, a weakling. *Modality* can result in nuance: certainly, probably, perhaps, probably not. Especially if synonymous characters have been discovered, these can mean a valuable refinement of the descriptive model.

Anyone who wishes to continue the investigation into the contents of the character further can examine the connections existing between the various characteristics. Are, for instance, certain sexes constantly combined with a certain ideological position? In many seventeenth- and eighteenth-century novels, a clear connection can be discerned between the male sex and a military ideology. There is, however, usually no connection in the same corpus between the female sex and a pacifist attitude. In female characters, the axis militarism-pacifism is thus not marked. The question arises, in relation to this, whether the fact that a certain character or group of characters (for instance, all the persons of one role) is not marked by a certain axis has any significance. It need not, in my view, be meaningful, but neither need it necessarily be meaningless. The fact that in seventeenth-century novels women did not take a clear stand either for or against war can certainly be regarded as significant: it indicates something about their (lack of) social position.

A character exhibits not only similarities to and differences from other characters. Often, there is a connection between the character, its situation, and its environment. This will be discussed later. For the moment, I wish only to point out the possibility of analysing the contents of a character and examining the connection with its environment more closely.

Finally, the description which has been obtained of a character can be contrasted with an analysis of the *functions* it performs in a series of events. See chapter 1. What kinds of actions does a character perform, and what role does it play in the fabula? This confrontation can yield information about the construction of the story with respect to the fabula. Because of a certain event, alterations may take place in the build-up of a character, and internal relations between the various characters may change. Conversely, alterations in the make-up of a character may influence events and determine the outcome of the fabula.

Sources of Information

The next question concerning the story which arises is the following: how do we come by our information about a character? There are two possibilities. Characteristics are either mentioned explicitly by the character itself, or we deduce them from what it does. Actually, we refer to a *qualification* when the information is given directly by a character. There are various possibilities for this. If a character talks about itself and to itself, it is practising self-analysis. We cannot be sure that it is judging itself correctly and literature shows many such cases: 'unreliable,' deceitful, too immature, incompetent, mentally disturbed self-analysts. The genres which are particularly well suited to this manner of qualification are obviously the autobiographical ones: diary, confession, autobiographical novel. In *The Tell-Tale Heart*, Edgar Allen Poe allows his character to explain why he is not insane, although he has murdered someone, and these confessions clearly demonstrate, because of their negation, the existence of his insanity. A character can talk about itself to others. It usually receives an answer, so that the qualification becomes plural in such a case, deriving from various sources. If one character says something about another character, this may or may not lead to a confrontation. The character under discussion may or may not be present. If it is, it can react, confirming or denying what has been said. If it is not, it may or may not already know what people think of it.

A third possibility for explicit qualification lies with a third party outside the fabula: the narrator makes statements about the character. This agent, too, may be a reliable or an unreliable judge. The party, for instance, which presents Dombey in Dickens' *Dombey and Son* as an entirely decent man is unreliable. Sometimes this presentation involves very obvious irony. When a character is presented by means of its actions, we may deduce from these certain implicit qualifications. Such an implicit, indirect qualification may be labelled a *qualification by function*. A deserter is thus qualified as a pacificist or a coward. A revolutionary who participates in a wild party qualifies as an epicurean or a hypocrite. Moreover, one character can do something to another that qualifies the latter, or that seduces it into qualifying itself. A detective who unmasks a murderer qualifies that character as a murderer. In that case, the qualification is explicit. But before the final arrest takes place the detective can lure his or her victim into a trap, so that the latter qualifies himself as a murderer. S/he can also, without words, push a gun to his chest, produce a piece of evidence and directly qualify him as a murderer.

If we now involve the various frequency possibilities as well, further differentiation becomes possible. Every qualification can be seen as either *singular* or *repetitive*. A singular qualification is always durative so that the frequency possibilities are restricted to two. The implicit qualification through action may be split up into *potential* actions (plans) and *realized* ones.

Summarizing: the difference between the first and the second category of information sources is that the first leads to explicit qualification and the second to implicit qualification. Explicit qualifications shed more light than implicit ones, but that light need not be reliable. Implicit, indirect qualifications can be interpreted differently by different readers, as in the case of the deserter. But implicit qualifications may also provide a means of uncovering lies and revealing secrets. See chapter 3, section 1.

On the basis of this investigation into sources of information, a division can be set up, classifying the character according to the degree of *emphasis* with which it is qualified. The *more ways* in which the qualification is communicated, the *oftener* a character is qualified, the more emphasis it receives. A conjunction with the number of semantic axes by which it is marked – that is, a classification of the character – may be achieved which is somewhat more plausible and more subtle than the current one based on *round* and *flat characters*.

For convenience' sake, I shall list the possible sources of information once again, this time in the form of a diagram. This diagram is no more than a summary of this paragraph. It is concerned only with the way in which information is given about a character. Every character we meet in a narrative can be placed in one of these twenty categories. In addition, such a character naturally occupies a place in, or with respect to, the actantial model in the semantic analysis. In principle, every possibility has thus been covered. It goes without saying that here too the investigators will determine how much effort they wish to invest in the description of a character.

The diagram should be read as follows. Every line gives one specific combination of the various data concerning the way in which the image of a character is presented. The possible combinations are indicated by numbers, the various aspects of the presentation by letters.

	a. method	b. frequency	c. subject-object	d. addressee	e. to/in presence of)	f. realization
1.	+	−	+	+	ϕ	ϕ
2.	+	+	+	+	ϕ	ϕ
3.	+	−	+	−	+	ϕ
4.	+	+	+	−	+	ϕ
5.	+	−	−	+	ϕ	ϕ
6.	+	+	−	+	ϕ	ϕ
7.	+	−	−	−	+	ϕ
8.	+	+	−	−	+	ϕ
9.	−	−	−	+	ϕ	−
10.	−	+	−	+	ϕ	−
11.	−	−	−	+	ϕ	+
12.	−	+	−	+	ϕ	+
13.	−	−	−	−	+	−
14.	−	+	−	−	+	−
15.	−	−	−	−	+	+
16.	−	+	−	−	+	+
17.	−	−	−	−	−	−
18.	−	+	−	−	−	−
19.	−	−	−	−	−	+
20.	−	+	−	−	−	+

a. explicit +; implicit −
b. singular −; repetitive +
c. character about itself +; character about another −
d. subject +; non-subject −
e. non-subject = object +; non-subject = non-object − (third character)
f. execution +; no execution − (plan)

The Problem of the Hero

From the very beginning of the study of literature, it has been customary to refer to the *hero* of a story. Who is the hero? This question is often asked. Usually, an intuitive choice is made.

Sometimes attempts are made to define the term *hero*, but these have not resulted in anything particularly concrete. The reader's ability to identify the hero was put forward as a criterion. But this differs, in many cases, from reader to reader. Another criterion has been suggested: the amount of moral approbation that the hero receives from the reader. Again, this varies with each reader and is difficult to determine. Nevertheless the history of literature offers examples of a development of the hero that seem to fulfil this moral requirement. Nineteenth-century heroes were characters who could survive in a hard and ruthless society, or who attempted to do so but failed. The existential hero is anti-bourgeois and politically committed. Questions concerning the identity of the hero are perhaps not relevant, but are raised so often that they warrant an attempt to formulate criteria by which a decision may be taken. Attempts have been made to define the term more clearly by naming a number of criteria according to which the hero could be rejected or the reader's intuitive choice could be explained. I shall mention these criteria briefly. Sometimes, the hero can also be equated, in many ways, with the *subject* (see chapter 3, section 1).

If the title of the hero or his or her explicit denomination does not clinch a decision, we can try and discover whether any one character distinguishes itself from the other characters in the following ways:

> qualification: comprehensive information about appearance, psychology, motivation, past
> distribution: the hero occurs often in the story, his or her presence is felt at important moments in the fabula
> independence: the hero can occur alone or hold monologues
> function: certain actions are those of the hero alone: s/he makes agreements, vanquishes opponents, unmasks traitors, etc.
> relations: s/he maintains relations with the largest number of characters

A distinction should be made, however, between the active, successful hero, the hero-victim, and the passive anti-hero (Tommy Wilhelm in Bellow's *Seize the Day*). The hero-victim will be confronted with opponents, but will not vanquish them. The anti-hero will hardly distinguish him- or herself by function, because s/he is passive. S/he will, however, meet all of the other four criteria.

The problem of the hero has ideological relevance, if only because of the connotations of the very concept. It is obvious that heroines display different features from male heroes, black from white heroes, in the large majority of the narratives. The suspicion that the choice of a hero and of the features attributed to him or her betrays an ideological position is a reason not to ignore the problem but rather to study it.

6   FROM PLACE TO SPACE

Few concepts deriving from the theory of narrative texts are as self-evident and have yet remained so vague, as the concept of *space*. Only a few theoretical publications have been devoted to it.

Place and Space

In chapter 1, section 5, I discussed *location* or *place* as an element of the fabula. There the term referred to the topological position in which the actors were situated and the events took place. The contrasts between locations and the borderlines between them were there viewed as predominant means of highlighting the significance of the fabula or even of determining it. In principle, places can be mapped out, in the same way that the topological position of a city or a river can be indicated on a map. The concept of *place* is related to the physical, mathematically measurable shape of spatial dimensions. Of course, in fiction, these places do not actually exist, as they do in reality. But our imaginative faculty dictates that they be included in the fabula.

The story is determined by the way in which the fabula is presented. During this process, places are linked to certain points of perception. These places seen *in relations to their perception* are called space. That point of perception may be a character, which is situated in a space, observes it, and reacts to it. An anonymous point of perception may also dominate the presentation of certain places. This distinction can result in a typology of spatial presentation. The general question concerning the various points of perception, which lies at the root of every presentation, will be discussed in section 7 of this chapter. In the investigation into narrative space, it is important to examine which aspects of space may be presented.

Spatial Aspects

There are three senses which are especially involved in the perception of space: *sight*, *hearing*, and *touch*. All three may result in the presentation of a space in the story. Usually shapes, colours, and sizes are perceived visually, always from a particular perspective. Sounds may contribute, though to a lesser degree, to the presentation of space. If a character hears a low buzz, it is probably still at a certain distance from the speakers. If it can understand word for word what is being said, then it is situated much nearer, in the same room, for instance, or behind a thin screen. A church clock sounding in the distance increases the space; suddenly perceived whispering points to the proximity of the whisperer. Thirdly, there is touch. Tactile perceptions usually have little spatial significance. Touch indicates adjacency. If a character feels walls on all sides, then it is confined in a very small space. Tactile perception is often used in a story to indicate the material, the substance of objects.

With the aid of these three senses two kinds of relations may be suggested between characters and space. The space in which the character is situated, or is precisely not situated, is regarded as the *frame*. The way in which that space is filled may also be indicated. A character can be situated in a space which it experiences as secure; while earlier on, outside that space, it felt insecure.

> a For hours, he wandered through the dark forest. All of a sudden, he saw a light. He hurried towards the house and knocked on the door. With a sigh of relief, he shut the door behind him a moment later.

Both inner and outer space function, in this instance, as a frame. Their opposition gives both spaces their meaning.

An inner space may also be experienced as unsafe, but with a somewhat different meaning. The inner space can, for instance, be experienced as confinement, while the outer space represents liberation and, consequently, security.

> b With a sigh of relief he presently closed the door behind himself. Free at last!

In both examples, the frame has a highly symbolic function. Naturally, this need not always be the case.

The filling in of space is determined by the objects that can be found in that space. Objects have spatial status. They determine the spatial effect of the room by their shape, measurements, and colours. After all, a cluttered room seems smaller, an empty room bigger than in fact it is. The way in which objects are arranged in a space, the configuration of objects, may also influence the perception of that space. In some stories, an object or objects are sometimes presented in detail. In other stories, space may be presented in a vague and implicit manner.

Content and Function

The semantic content of spatial aspects may be constructed in the same way as the semantic content of a character. Here, too, we find a preliminary combination of determination, repetition, accumulation, transformation, and the relations between various spaces.

Determination is again achieved on the basis of the reader's frame of reference. When a certain event is situated in Dublin, this will mean something different to the reader who is well acquainted with the city than to the reader who only knows that Dublin is a large city. The oppressive atmosphere of a dwelling in one of the poorer districts of Dublin is presented in a fairly detailed way in Joyce's *A Portrait of the Artist as a Young Man*. Those who are already familiar with that atmosphere will immediately be able to visualize much more, and for them the notations 'in the kitchen' and 'in the parlour' will evoke much more precise images.

Determination functions here too on the basis of the general application of characteristics. One big city has a number of characteristics in common with every big city. This also applies to the country, a village, a street, a house, and every general category. The more precise the presentation of a space the greater the amount of specific qualities added to the general ones, which then become steadily less dominating. But general characteristics never cease to function. Only by means of general characteristics is it possible to create an image at all.

Spaces function in a story in two ways. On the one hand, they are only a frame, a place of action. In this capacity a more or less detailed presentation will lead to a more or less concrete picture of that space. The space can also remain entirely in the background. In many cases, however, space is 'thematized': it becomes an object of presentation itself, for its own sake. Space thus becomes an 'acting place' rather than the place of action. It influences the fabula, and the fabula becomes subordinate to the presentation of space. The fact that 'this is happening here' is just as important as 'the way it is *here*,' which allows these events to happen. In both cases, where both frame-space and thematized space are concerned, space can function *steadily* or *dynamically*. A steady space is a fixed frame, thematized or not, within which the events take place. A dynamically functioning space is a factor which allows for the movement of characters. Characters walk, and therefore need a path. They travel, and so need a large space, countries, seas, air. The hero of a fairy tale has to traverse a dark forest to prove his courage. So there is a forest. That space is not present as a fixed frame, but as a passage to be taken, and can vary greatly. From a fast train, the traveller does not see the trees separately, but as one long mass. Space is indicated exactly for this reason, as a space in which the traveller is moving.

The movement of characters can constitute a transition from one space to another. Often, one space will be the other's opposite. A person is travelling, for instance, from a negative to a positive space. The space need not be the goal of that move. The latter may have quite a different aim, with space representing an important or an unimportant interim between departure and arrival, difficult or easy to traverse.

The character that is moving towards a goal need not always arrive in another space. In many travel stories, the movement is a goal in itself. It is expected to result in a change, liberation, introspection, wisdom, or knowledge.

If such an experiential aim is lacking, even implicitly, the movement, totally aimless, can function simply as a presentation of space. The move may be a circular one, the character returns to its point of departure. In this way, space is presented as a labyrinth, as unsafety, as confinement.

Relations to Other Elements

Relations between the various elements on the story level arise because of the way in which they are combined and presented. The relations between space and event become clear if we think of well-known, stereotypical combinations: declarations of love by moonlight on a balcony, high-flown reveries on a mountain-top, a rendezvous in an inn, ghostly appearances among ruins, brawls in cafés. In medieval literature, love-scenes frequently take place in a special space, appropriate to the occasion, the so-called *locus amoenus*, consisting of a meadow, a tree, and a running stream. Such a fixed combination is called a *topos*. In the literature of later periods, too, certain combinations occur which are sometimes characteristic of a writer, sometimes of a movement, and sometimes even of a novel. The expectation that a clearly marked space will function as the frame of a suitable event may also be disappointed.

The most obvious place to look for examples of the relations between space and character would seem to be the naturalistic novel, since it claims to depict the influence of the environment on man. A person's housing is especially connected to his character, his way of life, and his possibilities. In this sense, *A Portrait of the Artist as a Young Man* could also be regarded as naturalistic. Stephen Dedalus is obviously a product of impoverished circumstances. His way of life, his poor diet, his incessant scratching because of lice, his family's constant moves to ever-shabbier neighbourhoods are in complete accordance with the space in which he lives. The spatial position in which characters are situated at a certain moment often influences their mood. A space, situated high up, sometimes causes spirits to be high, so that the character is exalted (Stendhal). A highly situated space, where the character happens not to be, but which it is looking up to, or with which it is confronted in some other way, can depress it by its very inaccessibility (Kafka, *The Castle*).

The relationship between time and space is of importance for the rhythm. When a space is presented extensively, an interruption of the time sequence is unavoidable, unless the *perception* of the space takes place gradually (in time) and can therefore be regarded as an event. When a character enters a church to sightsee and the interior of the church is presented 'during' its tour, there is no interruption. Spatial indications are always *durative* (an extreme case of *iteration*). After all, a permanent object is always involved. In this sense, too, the chronology is always disrupted by spatial indications. Moreover, information concerning space is often repeated, to stress the stability of the frame, as opposed to the transitory nature of the events which occur within it. All these time-space relations belong to the categories discussed in sections 2 and 3 of this chapter.

Information

Finally, a few words about the way in which information concerning space is given. As I have said before, space is always *implicitly* necessary for every activity performed by a character. If a character is cycling, we know that it is outside and is riding on a path or a road. We know that it sleeps in a bed. In fact, if the information is added that it is sleeping soundly, then we may assume that the bed is warm and comfortable.

There are various ways of *explicitly* presenting information about space. Sometimes a very short indication, without details, is sufficient:

   c At home, John puts down the shopping-bag, with a sigh.

   d As soon as he had shut the door, John placed the shopping-bag underneath the hat-rack.

In *c* the indication of space is minimal; we only know that John is again inside, in his own home. Earlier presentations of that house will determine whether we are able to visualize in a more or less detailed way what the space is like in which he is situated. In *d* we know more, even if this indication is also quite brief. We know that, within the context of Western European floor plans, he is in the hall and that he has not, for instance, walked straight through to the kitchen. So probably he came in through the front door.

When separate sections of narrative are devoted to the presentation of information about space alone, we refer to *descriptions*. The space is then not simply indicated in passing, but is an explicit object of presentation.

I crossed the staircase landing, and entered the room she indicated. From that room, too, the daylight was completely excluded, and it had an airless smell that was oppressive. A fire had been lately kindled in the damp old-fashioned grate, and it was more disposed to go out than to burn up, and the reluctant smoke which hung in the room seemed colder than the clearer air – like our own marsh mist. Certainly wintry branches of candles on the high chimneypiece faintly lighted the chamber: or, it would be more expressive to say, faintly troubled its darkness. It was spacious, and I dare say had once been handsome, but every discernible thing in it was covered with dust and mould, and dropping to pieces. The most prominent object was a long table with a table-cloth spread on it, as if a feast had been in preparation when the

house and the clocks all stopped together. An épèrgne or centre-piece of some kind was in the middle of this cloth; it was so heav-ily overhung with cobwebs that its form was quite undistinguish-able; and, as I looked along the yellow expanse out of which I remember its seeming to grow, like a black fungus, I saw speckled-legged spiders with blotchy bodies running home to it, and run-ning out from it, as if some circumstance of the greatest public importance had just transpired in the spider community.
(Charles Dickens, *Great Expectations*)

This description is linked to the perception of the character: its elabo-rateness is motivated by the fact that that character is entering this space for the first time. Consequently, the boy is curious and takes in every detail. At the same time, he judges, which is announced in the second sentence. These aspects of the description – the point of per-ception, the motivation, and the relation between perception and opin-ion – will be discussed in section 7 of this chapter. For the moment, it is only important to note that, in such a fragment, space is presented explicitly, as an independent element. In some realistic novels, descrip-tions of space are executed with great precision. It is important that the realistic aspects in such descriptions be clearly visible: the space must resemble the actual world, so that the events situated within it also become plausible.

Finally, a space may be indicated explicitly, not because of an action taking place in it, but because of an action performed *with* it. An expression like 'walked into a wall' belongs to this category of indica-tions. People do walk into walls, literally and figuratively, if a space is too small, confined. Other examples are to scale a fence, to escape from prison, to lock someone in, to hide something, to clear a path through the jungle, to ascend to heaven, to go to hell. The effect of information about space is not only determined by the way in which it is conveyed. The *distance* from which the space is presented may also affect the image which emerges. If a space is presented from *far away*, an over-view of the whole is usually given, without details. Conversely, a space which is presented from nearby will be described in a detailed way, but the overview will be missing.

Both the image of a character and the image of a space which are offered to the reader are finally determined by the way in which the character and space are *seen*. The question 'Who is seeing?' must there-fore be the last aspect under discussion.

7   FOCALIZATION

Difficulties

Whenever events are presented, they are always presented from within a certain 'vision.' A point of view is chosen, a certain way of seeing things, a certain angle, whether 'real' historical facts are concerned or fictitious events. It is possible to try and give an 'objective' picture of the facts. But what does that involve? An attempt to present only what is seen or is perceived in some other way. All comment is shunned and implicit interpretation is also avoided. Perception, however, is a psychological process, strongly dependent on the position of the perceiving body; a small child sees things in a totally different way from an adult, if only as far as measurements are concerned. The degree to which one is familiar with what one sees also influences perception. When the Central American Indians first saw horsemen, they did not see the same things we do when we see people riding. They *saw* gigantic monsters, with human heads and four legs. These had to be gods. Perception depends on so many factors that striving for objectivity is pointless. To mention only a few factors: one's position with respect to the perceived object, the fall of the light, the distance, previous knowledge, psychological attitude towards the object; all this and more affects the picture one forms and passes on to others. In a story, elements of the fabula are presented in a certain way. We are confronted with a vision of the fabula. What is this vision like and where does it come from? These are the questions that will be discussed in these subsections. I shall refer to the relations between the elements presented and the vision through which they are presented with the term *focalization*. Focalization is, then, the relation between the vision and that which is 'seen,' perceived. By using this term I wish to dissociate myself from a number of current terms in this area, for reasons which I shall now explain.

   The theory of narration, as it has been developed in the course of this century, offers various labels for the concept here referred to. The most current one is *point of view* or *narrative perspective*. Narrative situation, narrative viewpoint, narrative manner are also employed. More or less elaborate typologies of 'narrative points of view' have been developed, of which I shall include the most well-known in my bibliography. All these typologies have proved more or less useful. They are all, however, unclear on one point. They do not make an explicit distinction

seeing ≠ narr^n

between, on the one hand, the vision through which the elements are presented and, on the other, the identity of the voice that is verbalizing that vision. To put it more simply: they do not make a distinction between _those who see_ and _those who speak_. Nevertheless, it is possible, both in fiction and in reality, for one person to express the vision of another. This happens all the time. When no distinction is made between these two different agents, it is difficult, if not impossible, to describe adequately the technique of a text in which something is seen – *and* that vision is narrated. The imprecisions of such typologies can sometimes lead to absurd formulations or classifications which are too rough-and-ready. To claim, as has been done, that Strether in Henry James' *The Ambassadors* is 'telling his own story,' whereas the novel is written 'in the third person,' is as nonsensical as to claim that the sentence:

a Elizabeth saw him lie there, pale and lost in thought.

is narrated, from the comma onwards, by the character Elizabeth; that means it is spoken by her. What this sentence does is to present Elizabeth's vision clearly: after all, she does *see* him lying down.

The existing typologies have achieved solid respectability in current literary criticism. There must be an explanation for this: their evident usefulness. All offer interesting possibilities, despite the objection just mentioned. I am of the opinion, however, that their distinctions should be adapted to the insight that the agent that sees must be given a status other than that of the agent that narrates.

If we examine the current terms from this point of view, only the term *perspective* seems clear enough. This label covers both the physical and the psychological points of perception. It does not cover the agent that is performing the action of narration, and it should not do so. Nevertheless, my own preference lies with the term *focalization* for two reasons and despite justly raised objections to the introduction of unnecessary new terminology. The first reason concerns tradition. Although the word 'perspective' reflects precisely what is meant here, it has come to indicate in the tradition of narrative theory both the narrator and the vision. This ambiguity has affected the specific sense of the word, in itself correct. If we were to use it here in a more specific sense, chances are that it would still be associated with the familiar, imprecise meaning.

There is yet another, more practical, objection to this term. No sub-

stantive can be derived from 'perspective' that could indicate the subject of the action; the verb 'to perspectivize' is not customary and
would, probably, if used, have another meaning than the one meant
here. In order to describe the focalization in a story we must have terms
such as these at our disposal. These two arguments seemed to me to be
weighty enough to justify my choice of a new term for a not completely
new concept. *Focalization* offers a number of extra, minor advantages
as well. It is a term that looks technical. It is derived from photography
and film; its technical nature is thus emphasized. As any 'vision' presented can have a strongly manipulative effect, and is, consequently,
very difficult to extract from the emotions, not only from those attributed to the focalizor and the character, but also from those of the
reader, a technical term will help us keep our attention on the technical side of such a means of manipulation.

The Focalizor

In Southern India, at Mahaballipuram, is what is said to be the largest
bas-relief of the world, the seventh-century *Arjuna's penance*. At the
upper left, the wise man Arjuna is depicted in a yoga position. At the
bottom right stands a cat. Around the cat are a number of mice. The
mice are laughing (see illustration). It is a strange image. Unless the
spectator interprets the signs. The interpretation runs as follows.
Arjuna is in a yoga position and is meditating to win Lord Siva's favour.
The cat, impressed by the beauty of absolute calm, imitates Arjuna.
Now the mice realize they are safe. They laugh. Without this interpretation, there is no relation between the parts of the relief. Within this
interpretation the parts form a coherent narrative.
    The picture is a comical one, in addition to being a real comic. The
comical effect is evoked by the narrativity of the picture. The spectator
sees the relief as a whole. Its contents include a succession in time.
First, Arjuna assumes the yoga position. Then, the cat imitates him.
After that, the mice start laughing. These three successive events are
logically related in a causal chain. According to every definition I know,
that means this is a fabula.
    But there is more. Not only are the events chronologically in succes-
sion and logically in a causal relation. They can only occur through the
semiotic activity of the actors. And the comical effect can only be
explained when this particular mediation is analysed. We laugh
because we can identify with the mice. Seeing what they see, we realize
with them that a meditating cat is a contradiction; cats hunt, and only

(drawing: Fransje van Zoest)

wise men meditate. Following the chain of events in reverse, we also arrive at the next one by perceptual identification. The cat has brought about the event for which he is responsible because he has seen Arjuna do something. This chain of perceptions also runs in time. The wise man sees nothing since he is totally absorbed in his meditation; the cat has seen Arjuna and now sees nothing more of this world; the mice see the cat *and* Arjuna. That is why they know they are safe. (Another interpretation is that the cat is simulating; this doesn't weaken my statements but only adds an element of suspense to the fabula.) The mice are laughing because of that very fact, finding the imitation a ridiculous enterprise. The spectator sees more. S/he sees the mice, the cat and the wise man. S/he laughs at the cat, and s/he laughs sympathetically with the mice, whose pleasure is comparable to that felt by a successful scoundrel.

This example, paradoxical because it is not linguistic, illustrates quite clearly the theory of focalization. We can view the picture of the relief as a (visual) sign. The elements of this sign, the standing Arjuna, the standing cat, the laughing mice, only have spatial relations to one another. The elements of the fabula – Arjuna assumes a yoga position, the cat assumes a yoga position, the mice laugh – do not form a coherent significance as such. The relation between the sign (the relief) and its contents (the fabula) can only be established by mediation of an interjacent layer, the view of the events. The cat sees Arjuna. The mice see the cat. The spectator sees the mice who see the cat who has seen Arjuna. And the spectator sees that the mice are right. Every verb of perception (*to see*) in this report indicates an activity of focalization. Every verb of action indicates an event.

Focalization is the relationship between the 'vision,' the agent that sees, and that which is seen. This relationship is a component of the story part, of the content of the narrative text: A says that B sees what C is doing. Sometimes that difference is void, e.g. when the reader is presented with a vision as directly as possible. The different agents then cannot be isolated, they coincide. That is a form of 'stream of consciousness.' Consequently, focalization belongs in the story, the layer in between the linguistic text and the fabula. Because the definition of focalization refers to a relationship, each pole of that relationship, the subject and the object of focalization, must be studied separately. The subject of focalization, the *focalizor*, is the point from which the elements are viewed. That point can lie with a character (i.e. an element of the fabula), or outside it. If the focalizor coincides with the character, that character will have a technical advantage over the other characters. The reader watches with the character's eyes and will, in principle, be inclined to accept the vision presented by that character. In Mulisch's *Massuro*, we see with the eyes of the character who later also draws up a report of the events. The first symptoms of Massuro's strange disease are the phenomena which the other perceives. These phenomena communicate Massuro's *condition* to us, they tell us nothing abut the way he feels about it. Such a character-bound focalizor, which we could label, for convenience' sake, CF, brings about *bias* and *limitation*. In Henry James' *What Maisie Knew* the focalization lies almost entirely with Maisie, a little girl who does not understand much about the problematic relations going on around her. Consequently, the reader is shown the events through the limited vision of the girl, and only gradually realizes what is actually going on. But the reader is not a little girl. S/he does more with the information s/he receives than Maisie does, s/he interprets it differently. Where Maisie sees only a strange gesture, the reader knows that s/he is dealing with an erotic one. The difference between the childish vision of the events and the interpretation that the adult reader gives to them determines the novel's special effect.

Character-bound focalization (CF) can vary, can shift from one character to another. In such cases, we may be given a good picture of the origins of a conflict. We are shown how differently the various characters view the same facts. This technique can result in neutrality towards all the characters. Nevertheless, there usually is never a doubt in our minds which character should receive most attention and sympathy. On the grounds of distribution, for instance the fact that a character focalizes the first and/or the last chapter, we label it the hero(ine) of the book.

When focalization lies with one character which participates in the fabula as an actor, we could refer to *internal* focalization. We can then indicate by means of the term *external* focalization that an anonymous agent, situated outside the fabula, is functioning as focalizor. Such an external, non-character-bound focalizor is abbreviated EF. In the following fragment from the opening of Doris Lessing's *The Summer before the Dark* we see the focalization move from EF to CF.

> *b* A woman stood on her back step, arms folded, waiting.
>   Thinking? She would not have said so. She was trying to catch hold of something, or to lay it bare so that she could look and define; for some time now she had been 'trying on' ideas like so many dresses off a rack. She was letting words and phrases as worn as nursery rhymes slide around her tongue: for towards the crucial experiences custom allots certain attitudes, and they are pretty stereotyped. A yes, first love! ... Growing up is bound to be painful! ... My first child, you know. ... But I was in love! ... Marriage is a compromise. ... I am not as young as I once was.

From sentence two onwards the contents of what the character experiences are given. A switch thus occurs from an external focalizor (EF) to an internal one (CF). An alternation between external and internal focalizors, between EF and CF, is visible in a good many stories. In *The Evenings*, Frits is the only character that functions as focalizor. Therefore, the two different focalizors are EF and CF-Frits. A number of characters can also alternate as CF focalizor; in that case, it can be useful to indicate the various characters in the analysis by their initials, so that one can retain a clear overview of the division of focalization: in Frits' case, this would mean the notation CF (Fr). An example of a story in which a great many different characters act as focalizor is *Of Old People*. However, the characters do not carry an equal load; some focalize often, others only a little, some do not focalize at all. It is also possible for the entire story to be focalized by EF. The narrative can then appear objective, because the events are not presented from the point of view of the characters. The focalizor's bias is, then, not absent, since there is no such thing as 'objectivity,' but it is unclear.

The Focalized Object

In *Of Old People* Harold is usually the focalizor when the events in the Indies are being focalized; Lot often focalizes his mother, mama Ottilie, and it is mainly because of this that we receive a fairly likeable image of her despite her unfriendly behaviour. Evidently, it is important to ascertain which character focalizes which object. The combination of a focalizor and a focalized object can be constant to a large degree (Harold-Indies; Lot-mama Ottilie), or it can vary greatly. Research into such fixed or loose combinations is of importance because the image we receive of the object is determined by the focalizor. Conversely, the image a focalizor presents of an object says something about the focalizor itself. Where focalization is concerned, the following questions are relevant.

1   *What* does the character focalize: what is it aimed at?
2   *How* does it do this: with what attitude does it view things?
3   *Who* focalizes it: whose focalized object is it?

What is focalized by a character F? It need not be a character. Objects, landscapes, events, in short all the elements are focalized, either by an EF or by a CF. Because of this fact alone, we are presented with a certain, far from innocent, interpretation of the elements. The degree to which a presentation includes an *opinion* can, of course, vary: the degree to which the focalizor points out its interpretative activities and makes them explicit also varies. Compare, for instance, the following descriptions of place:

c   Behind the round and spiny forms around us in the depth endless
    coconut plantations stretch far into the hazy blue distance where

mountain ranges ascended ghostlike. Closer, at my side, a ridged
and ribbed violet grey mountainside stretches upward with a sawtooth silhouette combing the white cloudy sky. Dark shadows of
the clouds lie at random on the slopes as if capricious dark-grey
pieces of cloth have been dropped on them. Close by, in a temple
niche, Buddha sits meditating in an arched window of shadow. A
dressing-jacket of white exudation of bird-droppings on his
shoulders. Sunshine on his hands which lie together perfectly at
rest.   (Jan Wolkers, *The Kiss*)

d Then we must first describe heaven, of course. Then the hundreds
of rows of angels arc clad in glorious shiny white garments. Everyone of them has long, slightly curly fair hair and blue eyes. There
are no men here. 'How strange that all angels should be women.'
There are no dirty angels with seductive panties, garterbelts and
stockings, not to mention bras. I always pictured an angel as a
woman who presents her breasts as if on saucers, with heavily
made-up eyes, and a bright red mouth, full of desire, eager to
please, in short, everything a woman should be. (Formerly, when I
was still a student, I wanted to transform Eve into a real whore. I
bought her everything necessary, but she did not want to wear the
stuff.)   (J.M.A. Biesheuvel, *The Way to the Light*, 'Faust')

In both cases, a CF is clearly involved; both focalizors may be localized
in the character 'I.' In *c*, the spatial position of the CF ('I') is especially
striking. It is obviously situated on a high elevation, considering the
wide prospect it has. The words 'around us,' combined with 'in the
depths,' stress that high position. The proximity of the niche with the
Buddha statue makes clear that CF ('I') is situated in an eastern temple
(the Burubudur in fact), so that 'the round and spiny form' (must) refer
to the temple roof. The presentation of the whole, temple roof and
landscape, seems fairly impersonal. If the CF ('I') had not been identified
itself by the use of the first-person personal pronoun in 'at my side' and
'around us,' this would have seemed, on the face of it, an 'objective' description, perhaps taken from a pamphlet or a geography book.
   On closer analysis, this proves not to be the case. Whether the CF ('I')
is explicitly named or not, the 'internal' position of the focalizor is, in
fact, already established by expressions such as 'close by,' 'closer,' and 'at
my side,' which underline the vicinity between the place and the per-
ceiver. 'Behind' and 'far into' indicate a specification of the spatial per-

spective (in the pictorial sense). But more happens here. Without appearing to do so, this presentation *interprets*. This is clear from the use of metaphors, which points to the facts that the CF ('I') attempts to reduce the objects it sees, which impress it a great deal, to human, everyday proportions. In this way, the CF ('I') is undoubtedly trying to fit the object into its own realm of experience. Images like 'sawtooth' and 'combing,' 'capricious dark-grey pieces of cloth,' and clichés like 'mountain ranges' bear this out. The 'dressing-jacket of white exudation of bird-droppings' is the clearest example. Actually, the image is also interesting because of the association mechanism it exhibits. With the word 'dressing-jacket,' the Buddhas statue becomes human, and as soon as it is human, the white layer on its head could easily be dandruff, a possibility suggested by the word 'exudation.' The realistic nature of the presentation – CF ('I') does 'really' *see* the landscape – is restored immediately afterwards by the information about the real nature of the white layer: bird-droppings. Thus, what we see here is the presentation of a landscape which is realistic, reflecting what is actually perceived, and at the same time interpreting the view in a specific way, so that it can be assimilated by the character.

Example *d* exhibits to a certain extent the same characteristics. Here, too, an impressive space is humanized. However, the CF ('I') observes the object less and interprets it more. It concerns a fantasy object with which the CF ('I') is sketchily familiar from religious literature and painting, but which it can adapt as much as it wishes, to its own taste. This is what it does, and its taste is clear. Here, too, an association mechanism is visible. From the traditional image of angels, implied in the second or third sentence, the CF ('I') moves to the assumption that angels are women. In this, the vision already deviates from the traditional vision, in which angels are asexual or male. Against the image thus created of asexual male angels, the CF ('I') sets up, in contrast, its own female image, which by now has moved very far away from the image that we have of angels.

And even before the reader realizes that in doing so a link is made with another tradition, that of the opposition angel-whore, in which 'angel' is used in a figurative sense, the word 'whore' itself appears in the text. In this, the interpretive mode of the description manifests itself clearly. The solemn 'we' of the beginning contrasts sharply with the personal turn which the description takes. The humour is here based on the contrast between the solemn-impersonal and the personal-everyday. The interpretive focalization is emphasized in several ways.

The sentence in quotation marks is presented as a reaction to the sentence preceding it. Here, the interpreting focalizor makes an explicit entrance. Later this is stressed again: 'not to mention' is a colloquial expression, and points at a personal subject, expressing an opinion: 'I always pictured an angel as ...' accentuates even more strongly that a personal opinion is involved.

The way in which a subject is presented gives information about that object itself and about the focalizor. These two descriptions give even more information about the CFs ('I') than about the object; more about the way they experience nature (c) or women (d), respectively, than about the Burubudur temple and heaven. In principle, it doesn't matter whether the object 'really exists' in actuality, or is part of a fictitious fabula, or whether it is a fantasy created by the character and so a doubly fictitious object. The comparison with the object referred to served in the above analysis only to motivate the interpretation by the CF ('I') in both fragments. The internal structure of the descriptions provides in itself sufficient clues about the degree to which one CF ('I') showed similarity to and differed from the other.

These two examples indicate yet another distinction. In c the object of the focalization was perceptible. The CF ('I') 'really' sees something that is outside itself. This is not always the case. An object can also be visible only inside the head of the CF. And only those who have access to it can perceive anything. This cannot be another character, at least not according to the classical rules of the narrative genre, but it might possibly be an EF. Such a 'non-perceptible' object occurs in cases where, for instance, the contents of a character's dream are presented. Concerning the heaven in d, we can only decide whether that object is perceptible or not perceptible when we know how the fragment fits into its context. If the 'I,' together with another person – a devil, for instance – is on an excursion to heaven, we will have to accept the first part of the description, until the sentence in quotation marks, as 'perceptible.' Thus, our criterion is that within the fabula there must be another character present that can also perceive the object; if they are the dreams, fantasies, thoughts, or feelings of a character, then these objects can be part of the category 'non-perceptible' objects. This distinction can be indicated by adding to the notation of the focalizor a 'p' or an 'np.' For b we end up with CF (woman)-np; for c, CF('I')-p, and for d, CF ('I')-np. This distinction too is of importance for an insight into the power-structure between the characters. When in a conflict situation one character is allotted both CF-p and CF-np, and the other exclusively

CF–p, then the first character has the advantage as a party in the conflict. It can give the reader insight into its feelings and thoughts, while the other character cannot communicate anything. Moreover, the other character will not have the insight which the reader receives, so that it cannot react to the feelings of the other (which it does not know), cannot adapt itself to them or oppose them. Such an inequality in position between characters is obvious in the so-called 'first-person novels,' but in other kinds this inequality is not always as clear to the reader. Yet the latter is manipulated by it in forming an opinion about the various characters. Consequently, the focalization has a strongly manipulative effect. Colette's novel *La Chatte* is a strong case: the reader is manipulated by this device into taking the man's side against his wife.

In this respect, it is important to keep sight of the difference between spoken and unspoken *words* of the characters. Spoken words are audible to others and are thus perceptible when the focalization lies with someone else. Unspoken words – thoughts, internal monologues – no matter how extensive, are not perceptible to other characters. Here, too, lies a possibility for manipulation which is often used. Readers are given elaborate information about the thoughts of a character, which the other characters do not hear. If these thoughts are placed in between the sections of dialogue, readers do not often realize how much less the other character knows than they do. An analysis of the perceptibility of the focalized objects supplies insight into these objects' relationships.

Levels of Focalization

Compare the following sentences:

e Mary participates in the protest march.

f I saw that Mary participated in the protest march.

g Michele saw that Mary participated in the protest march.

In all three sentences it is stated that Mary participated in the protest march. That is a clearly perceptible fact. We assume that there is an agent which is doing the perceiving, and whose perceptions are being presented to the reader. In f this is an 'I,' in g it is Michele. In e no party is indicated. Consequently, we assume that there is an external focalizor situated outside the fabula. This could be an EF or a CF ('I'), which remains implicit in this sentence but manifests itself elsewhere. We can thus analyse:

e EF–p

f CF ('I')–p

g CF (Michele)–p

The dash indicates the relation between the subject and the object of focalization. However, the difference between these sentences has not yet been expressed completely. Sentences *f* and *g* are complex sentences. The focalization, too, is complex. The analysis, as it is given here, only applies to the subordinate clause. In *f* it is stated that 'I' saw, and in *g* that Michele saw. Who focalized that section? Either an EF or a CF. We can only conclude that from the rest of the story. For *f* the possibilities are:

1 EF–[np CF ('I')–p]: an external focalizor focalizes the CF ('I'), which sees. 'Seeing' is a non-perceptible action, in contrast to 'looking,' so the complex focalized object is np. That object consists itself of a focalizor, CF ('I'), which sees something that is perceptible.

2 CF ('I')–[np CF ('I')–p], a so-called 'first-person narrative,' in which the external focalizor remembers afterwards that at a certain moment in the fabula, it saw Mary participating in a protest march.

The first possibility exists in theory, but will not easily occur, unless the sentence is in direct speech, and the CF ('I') can be identified as one of the persons speaking (temporarily). In *g* only the first formula is possible: EF–[np CF (Michele)–p]. This is easy to see once we realize that a personal focalizor cannot perceive a non-perceptible object, unless it is part of that object, is the same 'person'.

Two conclusions can be drawn from this. Firstly, it appears that various focalization *levels* can be distinguished; secondly, where the *focalization level* is concerned, there is no fundamental difference between a 'first-person narrative' and a 'third-person narrative.' When EF seems to 'yield' focalization to a CF, what is really happening is that the vision of the CF is being given within the all-encompassing vision of the EF. In fact, the latter always keeps the focalization in which the focalization of a CF may be embedded as object. This too is explicable in terms of the general principles of narratology. When we try to reflect someone else's point of view, we can only do so in so far as we know and understand that point of view. That is why there is no difference in focalization between a so-called 'first-person narrative' and a 'third-person narrative.' I will come back to this question in chapter 3. In a so-called 'first-person narrative' too an external focalizor, usually the 'I' grown older, gives its vision of a fabula in which it participated earlier as an actor, from the outside. At some moments it can present the vision of its younger alter ego, so that a CF is focalizing on the second level.

One remark about the notation of these data. If we wish to include the question of levels in the analysis, we can do so in an elaborate manner, as I have done here. That is useful if we wish to know what the relationship between the various focalizors is like: who allows whom to watch whom? If, however, we are only concerned with the relationship between the subject and the object of the focalization – for instance, in f between CF ('I') and Mary, or in g between CF (Michele) and Mary – then it is easier to remind ourselves of the fact that we are dealing with an embedded focalization, because at any moment the narrative may return to the first level. In that case, it is simple to indicate the level with a number following the F. for f this would be: CF2 ('I')–p and for g CF2 (Michele)–p.

If we summarize briefly what has preceded, it appears that the three sentences each differ one from another, in various ways. There is always *one* sentence which differs from the other two. Thus e differs from f and g in focalization level. Consequently focalization in e is singular and in f and g it is complex. And e and f differ from g as far as 'person' is concerned. In both cases it can be an EF or a CF ('I'). Finally, e and g differ from f because in f an EF cannot simply be assumed without doubt. This is only possible if the sentence is in direct speech.

We assume, therefore, a first level of focalization (F1) at which the focalizor is external. This external focalizor delegates focalization to an internal focalizor, the focalizor on the second level (F2). In principle there are more levels possible. In these sample sentences it is clear *where* the focalization is transferred from the first to the second level. The verb form 'saw' indicates that. Such markers of shifts in level we call *coupling signs.* There are signs which indicate the shift from one level to another. These signs can remain implicit. Sometimes we are forced to deduce them from other, less clear information. In example c, the description of the view on *and* from the Burubudur, we needed the preceding passage to find the sign with which the shift was indicated explicitly. In *d* a whole sentence – "Then we must first describe heaven of course" – is used to indicate that the internal CF is now going to give its own vision of heaven. Verbs like 'see' and 'hear,' in short all verbs that communicate perception, can function as explicit coupling signs.

There is yet another possibility. The external EF can also *watch along with* a person, without leaving focalization entirely to a CF. This happens when an object (which a character can perceive) is focalized, but nothing clearly indicates whether it is actually perceived. This procedure is comparable to free indirect speech, in which the narrating party approximates as closely as possible the character's own words without letting it speak directly (see chapter 3). An example of such a 'free indirect' focalization, or rather, ambiguous focalization, is the beginning of the story 'Lady with Lapdog' by Chekhov:

> *h* 1 The appearance on the front of a new arrival – a lady with a lapdog – became the topic of general conversation. 2 Dmitri Dmitrich Gurov, who had been a fortnight in Yalta and got used to its ways, was also interested in new arrivals. 3 One day, sitting on the terrace of Vernet's restaurant, he saw a young woman walking along the promenade; she was fair, not very tall, and wore a toque; behind her trotted a white pomeranian.
>
> 4 Later he came across her in the park and in the square several times a day. 5 She was always alone, always wearing the same toque, followed by the white pomeranian, no one knew who she was, and she became known simply as the lady with the lapdog.

This fragment as a whole is focalized by an external EF. In the third sentence a shift of level takes place, indicated by the verb 'to see.' In sentence 4, level one has been restored. But in sentence 5 it is ambivalent. This sentence follows the one in which it was stated that Dmitri meets the lady regularly. The description of the lady which follows would, according to our expectation, have to be focalized by that character: CF2 (Dmitri)-p, but there is no indication which signals that change of level. In the second part of the sentence focalization clearly rests again with EF1. The first part of sentence 5 may be focalized both by EF1 as by CF2. Such a double focalization, in which EF 'looks over the shoulder' of CF, we may indicate with the double notation EF1/CF2. Such a part of the story might be called *hinge*, a fragment with a double, or at any rate ambiguous, focalization in between two levels. It is also possible to distinguish between *double* focalization, which can be represented as EF1+CF2, and *ambiguous* focalization, in which it is hard to decide who focalizes: EF1/CF2. In *h* this difference cannot be established. In view of the development of the rest of the story EF1+CF2 seems most likely.

Suspense

As a conclusion to this chapter, a few remarks about suspense. Suspense is a frequent fact of experience, difficult to analyse. In so far as suspense is a psychological process, nothing need be said about it here. If, however, we define suspense as the results of the procedures by which the reader or the character is made to ask questions which are only answered later, it is possible in terms of focalization to get some grasp of the various kinds of suspense.

These questions may be asked and answered within a short space of time, or only at the end of the story. It is also possible that some questions are solved fairly quickly, while others are shelved. If suspense is to develop, then the questions will, somehow, be recalled repeatedly. In the paragraphs dealing with order, it was noticed that suspense can be generated by the announcement of something that will occur later, or by temporary silence concerning information which is needed. In both cases, the image which is presented to the reader is manipulated. That image is given by the focalizor. In principle, it coincides with the image that the focalizor has itself: the latter has been compared to a camera, after all. But the focalizor's image can be incomplete. This is the case when the characters 'know' mor than the focalizor. That 'knowing more' must, of course, appear later. It is also possible for the focalizor to falsify an image by, for instance, leaving out certain elements, hiding them from the reader. In such a case, the characters also 'know more' than the reader. The focalizor can also be in the possession of information which the characters do not know; for instance, about the origins of events. Then the reader, along with the focalizor, knows more than the character. The reader can thus receive an image that is just as complete or incomplete, more complete or less complete than the image the characters have of themselves. The focalizor determines that. If we now attempt to analyse suspense according to the 'knowledge' of reader and character on the basis of information provided through the focalizor, four possibilities emerge.

When a question is raised (who did it? what happened? how will it end?) it is possible that neither the reader nor the character can answer it. This is the opening situation of almost every detective novel. It is also possible that the reader does know the answer, but the character does not. The tension, in this case, is different. The question is not what the answer will be but whether the character will discover it for itself in time. This is the suspense that lies at the root of a threat. A character makes a mistake. Will it realize this in time? There is someone standing behind it with an axe. Will it turn round in time? Conversely, it can also be the case that the reader does not know the answer and the characters do, as in *Of Old People*. The answer can then be gradually revealed, in various phases and by means of various focalizors (Harold, the old people themselves, and the others, each one according to its own knowledge), or in the form of a puzzle, if the information is revealed, but is not marked as data, as in a detective novel. When, finally, reader and character are both informed of the answer, there is no suspense. Schematically expressed, when a question is evoked, the possibilities that the answer is known are thus:

> reader – character – (riddle, detective story, search)
> reader + character – (threat)
> reader – character + (secret, for instance *Of Old People*)
> reader + character + (no suspense)

In each of these forms of suspense one might analyse in turn, if necessary, which character knows the answer, and through which channel of focalization (EF1, CF2?) the reader learns the answer.

8   REMARKS AND SOURCES

Most of the topics that have been discussed in this chapter are part of the traditional 'theory of the novel.' In various countries, at various periods in the history of literary theory, and according to various principles, concepts have been developed, often independently of each other, which were presented under the deceptive title 'theory of the novel.' This title is deceptive for two reasons. The *novel* is probably the most heavily researched textual form. The concepts and distinctions that have emerged from this research usually have a more general scope. In so far as genre distinctions were taken into account, the novel was in these studies contrasted sometimes with drama, sometimes with poetry, and sometimes with the novella or short story. By using the term 'theory of the novel' to indicate sometimes (but not always) a much larger area of narratology, critics obscured the precise position of the novel with respect to other genres and types of text. Consequently, it is sometimes difficult to see to which area distinctions apply.

In the second place, the term 'theory of the novel' is deceptive because there can be no system as is presupposed by the term 'theory.' As I said, work was done in very different contexts on various components of the 'theory of the novel.' We have already seen that Müller and his disciples concerned themselves with the temporal relationships in the novel. In Anglo-Saxon countries work was done at another time, primarily on 'point of view' theories. Müller worked with technical, quantitative criteria. The 'point of view' theories were based mainly on psychological criteria. It seems difficult to imagine that these two groups of investigators were working on the same theory. Before reference could be made to a *theory*, all those different distinctions and concepts had to be brought together in *one* system.

One attempt to place all the traditional narratological distinctions together within one systematic, theoretical framework is formed by Genette's 'Discours du récit' (Genette, 1972). He joins the different time aspects and focalization in one frame, in which he also places the narrative text.

The highly different origins of the various aspects made it difficult to allot them all a place in a systematic theory of the story level. I have tried to solve this problem by retaining a clear point of departure. That point of departure was the question how information about the fabula is presented to the reader. The more technical aspects within this framework (such as various time aspects) could be placed, but so could aspects such as the image of a character and space. Here the questions were specified: what kind of information do we get? how do we get it? how do the various elements and aspects function in relation to each other?

That last question as to how the elements and aspects function is finally determined by focalization. Focalization is a central concept in this chapter. It has an 'overarching' position with respect to the other aspects. The significance of certain aspects cannot be viewed unless it is linked to focalization. Moreover, focalization is, in my view, the most important, most penetrating, and most subtle means of manipulation. Analyses of newspaper reports which aim at revealing the hidden ideology embedded in such reports should involve focalization in their investigation, and not restrict themselves to so-called *content analysis*, i.e. the semantic analysis of content. It is regrettable and, perhaps significant that, with regard to this crucial, so often neglected aspect, no single distinction has been sufficiently developed and formulated unambiguously. This is probably to be blamed on the vaguely psychological way in which these problems have been viewed.

It is therefore necessary, precisely where this topic is concerned, to break with tradition and design new criteria for distinction, new terms, and new descriptive methods.

The theory of the anachrony has been further developed since Lämmert in 1955 first made an extensive study of it. The most systematic exposition of this subject, and of the other time aspects too, has until today been that of Genette (1972). Genette considers every variation on a set pattern a (rhetorical) figure, an attitude which is reflected in the title of his book *Figures III*. Within the framework of that theory, it is understandable that he sought to express such figures in terms which would fit into the technical terminology derived from Greek rhetoric. Since such terms, which do indeed have advantages, appear rather cryptic and, consequently, tend to repel, I attempted to avoid them, and at most mentioned them in conjunction with English terms, unless no adequate English term could be found. Actually, Genette's terms are not really as difficult as they appear, because they have been systematically constructed out of several prepositions and the stems of words. For those who wish to use them in further analysis, it is perhaps useful to know how they are structured. The prepositions are *ana* and *pro*, which mean, respectively, 'towards/from the back' and 'towards/in the front.' *Para* means 'to the side.' The stem *lips* means 'leaving something out' and *leps*, 'adding something.' Thus, we end up with for instance, *paralips* in the sense of 'something is left out on the side (a missing side-track),' and *paraleps*: 'something is added to the side.' For Genette's complete time theory, I refer the reader to the English translation of his work (1980).

The article by Hamon (1977) (from which I have borrowed a great deal in this chapter) deals with characters. In this article, Hamon treats the most important aspects of the characters, and places them in a semiotic framework. His later book (1983) is based on the same model. His division of the characters into signifier and signified I find problematic.

Booth discusses the unreliable narator (1961). The best-known study of space is still the philosophically and psychoanalytically tinted *Poetics of Space* by Bachelard. Uspenski (1973) broaches interesting aspects of this problem. Lodge discusses a series of location descriptions, which are, in his view, progressively more poetic.

Friedman's typology of narrative points of view (1955) is based on various criteria (amount of information, 'perspective,' identity and attitude of the narrator) and is, consequently, less systematic than could be wished. The same goes for Booth's well-known fifth chapter. Both contain, however, a good many interesting insights. The distinction between narration and focalization is introduced by Genette (1972). A critical discussion, and a theoretical justification of the ideas presented here, may be found in Bal (1984). A good survey of narratology, which is also based on a (somewhat different) distinction of three layers and which discusses focalization and character interestingly, is provided by Rimmon-Kenan (1983). Lanswer's use of the term 'focalization' is somewhat loose (1982). I owe the remarks concerning suspense to suggestions offered by my colleague Wim van den Berg.

3

Text: Words

1 PRELIMINARY REMARKS

A narrative text is a text in which a narrative agent tells a story. Earlier
in the book I gave this as definition of the textual layer. In this chapter,
the different aspects of this definition will be further explained. The
first question which arises is that of the identity and status of the
narrative agent. Before we can begin discussing this, however, it is
necessary to place this concept in relation to some neighbouring
though different concepts. When, in this chapter, I discuss the narrative agent, or *narrator*, I mean the linguistic subject, a function and not
a person, which expresses itself in the language that constitutes the
text. It hardly needs mentioning that this agent is not the (biographical) author of the narrative. The narrator of *Emma* is not Jane Austen.
The historical person Jane Austen is, of course, not without importance for literary history, but the circumstances of her life are of no
consequence to the specific discipline of narratology. In order to keep
this distinction in mind, I shall refer to the narrator as *it*, however odd
this may seem.

In speaking of the narrator, I also do not mean the so-called '*implied
author*.' Since this term is used rather often, I think it best to devote a
few words to it. The term was introduced by Booth (1961) in order to
discuss and analyse the ideological and moral stances of a narrative
text without having to refer directly to a biographical author. In Booth's
use of the term, it denotes the totality of meanings that can be inferred

from a text. Thus the *implied author* is the *result* of the investigation of the meaning of a text, and not the *source* of that meaning. Only after interpreting the text on the basis of a text description can the implied author be inferred and discussed.

Moreover, the notion of an *implied author* is, in this sense, not limited to narrative texts, but is of application to any text. This is why the notion is not specific to narratology, which has, as I said before, as its objective the narrative aspects of a narrative text.

The notion of the *narrator* needs still further placement, however. We also do not mean a story-teller, a visible, fictive 'I' who interferes in his/her account as much as s/he likes, or even participates as a character in the action. Such a 'visible' narrator is a specific version of the narrator, one of the several different possibilities of manifestation. In this chapter, we shall rigorously stick to the definition of 'that agent which utters the linguistic signs which constitute the text.' Only if we confine ourselves to this definition can we avoid confusion.

2   THE NARRATOR

There are two reasons for beginning this chapter with the narrator. The narrator is the most central concept in the analysis of narrative texts. The identity of the narrator, the degree to which and the manner in which that identity is indicated in the text, and the choices that are implied lend the text its specific character. Moreover, this topic is closely related to the notion of focalization, with which it has, traditionally, been identified. Narrator and focalization together determine what has been called *narration* – incorrectly, because only the narrator narrates, i.e. utters language which may be termed narrative since it represents a *story*. If we see focalization as part of narration, we fail to make a distinction between linguistic, i.e. textual, agents and the purpose, the object, of their activity, and therefore might as well regard all the topics discussed so far as belonging to narrative technique, or, at any rate, all the topics in chapter 2. *Narrative technique* has, in that case, a wider meaning. It denotes 'all techniques used to tell a story.' In that case we might call the elaboration of an actant to a specific character 'narrative technique' with no less justification than the focalization of that character.

The fact that 'narration' has always implied focalization may be related to the notion that language shapes vision and world-view, rather than the other way around. That idea will not be discussed here, since it would carry us too far. But as far as it implies that language can be isolated from its object only artificially, *for the duration of the analysis,* that idea may very well be squared with the practice endorsed here. After all, as I said in the introduction, the separation into several layers is only temporarily meaningful, and has as its purpose a better insight into the functioning of the extremely complex meaning of the narrative text. If one proceeds to layering, one must do so analytically. And doing so, one will inevitably arrive at the conclusion that *seeing,* taken in the widest sense, constitutes the object of *narrating.*

This is, emphatically, not to say that the narrator should not be analysed in relation to the focalizing agent. On the contrary, precisely when the connection between these two agents is *not* self-evident, one may the more easily gain insight into the complexity of the relationship between the three agents that function in the three layers – the actor, the focalizor, the the narrator – and those moments at which they do or do not overlap in the shape of a single 'person.'

'I' and 'He' Are Both 'I'

To what does the distinction between first-person and third-person novels refer? Let us first consider *Of Old People.*

   a Steyn's deep bass resounded in the vestibule.

In this sentence we may distinguish:

1 An event in an (in this case fictitious) fabula: the sounding of a voice belonging to Steyn.
2 Someone who hears the voice resound, who is sensitive to the timbre of that voice and to the specific (hollow) resonance that sounds acquire in a vestibule.
3 A speaking agent that names the event and its perception.

The speaking agent does not mention itself in the process. It might just as well have done so. Then we would have read: '(I narrate:) Steyn's deep bass resounded in the vestibule.' This does not change anything in the analysis given above. In principle, it does not make a difference *to the status of the narration* whether a narrator refers to itself or not. As soon as there is language, there is a speaker who utters it; as soon as those linguistic utterances constitute a narrative text, there is a narrator, a narrating subject. From a grammatical point of view, this is *always* a 'first person.' In fact, the term 'third-person narrator' is absurd: a narrator is not a 'he' or 'she.' At best the narrator can narrate *about* someone else, a 'he' or 'she.' Of course, this does not imply that the distinction between 'first-person' and 'third-person' narratives is invalid. Just compare the following sentences:

   b I shall be twenty-one tomorrow.

   c Elizabeth will be twenty-one tomorrow.

If what I said above is valid, we may rewrite both sentences as:

   (I say:) I shall be twenty-one tomorrow.

   (I say:) Elizabeth will be twenty-one tomorrow.

Both sentences are uttered by a speaking subject, an 'I.' The difference rests in the object of the utterance. In *b* the 'I' speaks about itself. In *c* the 'I' speaks about someone else. When in a text the narrator never refers explicitly to itself as a character, we may, again, speak of an external narrator (EN). After all, it does not figure in the fabula. On the other hand, if the 'I' is to be identified with a character in the fabula it itself narrates, we may speak of a character-bound narrator, a CN.

This difference between an EN and a CN, a narrator that tells about others and a narrator that tells about itself, *may* relate to a difference in narrative intention. A CN usually proclaims that it recounts true facts about itself. It may pretend to be writing its autobiography. Its narrative intention may, if it is clear, be indicated by the addition:

autobiog.

   (I narrate: (I state autobiographically:)) I felt somewhat tired that day.

The intention of an EN may also be to present a story about others as true. We may indicate this as follows:

   (I narrate: (I testify:)) Elizabeth felt somewhat tired that day.

On the other hand, the intention may be to point to the presence of invention. Indications that the narrator's intention is to tell a fictive story are, for instance, generic indications such as 'Once upon a time ...,' which is often present at the beginning of a fairy tale, and subtitles such as 'A Novel' or 'A Winter's Tale.' These indications suggest *fictionality*. The fabula is fictitious, invented.

All Kinds of 'I's

Compare the following passages, of which only *d* is from Couperus' novel.

   d Steyn's deep bass resounded in the vestibule.
– Come Jack, come dog, come along with your boss! Are you coming? The happy bark of the terrier resounded. Up and down on the stairs stormed his enthusiastic speed, as if tripping over his own paws.
– Oh, that voice of Steyn's! mama Ottilie hissed between her teeth, and she angrily turned the pages in her book.

   e I sat quietly dozing in the room. But, again, I was not allowed to remain so. Hardly had I sat there five minutes when there it was again. Steyn's deep bass resounded in the vestibule. Oh, that voice of Steyn's!

   f One day a gentleman, whom I shall, for simplicity's sake, call Steyn, went for a walk with his dog, while his wife sat dozing in the room. Steyn's deep bass resounded in the vestibule. She started at his voice, because she is very sensitive to sounds. Oh, that voice of Steyn's!

   g Though Steyn assured me repeatedly that he only went out to walk his dog, his wife remained convinced that he kept a mistress. Every time he went out, she was irritated. One day it happened again. Steyn's deep bass resounded in the vestibule. Oh, that voice of Steyn's!

If we compare the relationship between the narrative 'I' and what is narrated in these four fragments, we may contrast *d* and *f* with *e* and *g*. The 'I,' the narrative subject in *d* and *f*, is not a character in the story it narrates, while the narrator of *e* and *g* is also a character. Looking at example *a*, we note that the sentence that this example consists of recurs unchanged in all four fragments. In each we have:

1   an event in a fabula: the sounding of Steyn's voice
2   someone who hears the sound of that voice, and – it appears – is irritated
3   a speaking agent, which names the event *and* its perception

In *d*, as we can say now we have full information, the voice belongs to the character Steyn; the perception, i.e. the irritation, belongs to Steyn's wife Ottilie; and the speaking agent is an EN. Since we are dealing with a novel, we may expect that the fabula is invented, but this is of minor importance here. Now we may interpret the sentence like this: (I narrate: (I invent: (Ottilie focalizes:))) Steyn's deep bass resounded in the vestibule. If we want to indicate briefly how the sentence works, we might also formulate it like this: EN [CF (Ottilie)–Steyn(p)]. The narrator, the focalizor, and the actor are each of different identity: the narrator is EN, the focalizor is Ottilie, and the actor is Steyn.

In *e* we apparently have a narrator whose intention it is to relate the events of her own life in a story which will explain its eventual outcome (let us assume a divorce). We may interpret the sentence like this: (I narrate: (I state autobiographically in order to explain:)) Steyn's deep bass resounded in the vestibule. This sentence relates the event caused by the actor Steyn, its perception by the focalizor 'I,' and the narrative act by the narrator 'I'; both those 'I's are called Ottilie. Thus we have: CN (Ott.) [CF (Ott.)–Steyn(p)]. Two of the three agents have the same name and the same identity.

In *f* the situation is different again. The word 'I' appears in the text. The narrator names itself. But it is not a character in the fabula. Still, it does more than just refer to its identity as an 'I.' A sentence like 'because she is very sensitive to sounds' presents itself as an explanation which might even denote partiality, though we cannot decide on the basis of this brief fragment. The sensitivity mentioned may constitute an accusation of Steyn, who takes insufficient account of it. On the other hand, it may constitute an accusation of Ottilie, who is hypersensitive. Let us, temporarily, choose the first interpretation. Then we have a case of double focalization, that of the anonymous focalizor which may be located in the narrative agent, and that of the character to which it is partial: EF [CF (Ott.)]–Steyn(p), or, with an indication of the levels of focalization: EF1 [CF2 (Ott.)]–Steyn(p). The fact that the focalization cannot reside exclusively with the EN is apparent from the sentence that follows 'Steyn's deep bass resounded in the vestibule': Ottilie, after all, started at the sound of Steyn's voice. Supposing again that this fragment is taken from a novel, we take it as fictional. But the intention may be to explain situations like the one disclosed in that novel in more general terms, hence the partiality signalled above. Thus we have: (I narrate (I invent with the intention to explain:)) Steyn's deep bass sounded in the vestibule.

We must now take into account the fact that the narrator manifests itself in its text, refers to itself as 'I,' while we must also think of the fact that that 'I' is not a character, not an actor as in *e*. This case may be indicated by the addition of the term 'perceptible' or 'non-perceptible,' with which we mean, of course, perceptible (p) or non-perceptible (np) as specifically mentioned agent in the text. The formula for that sentence might then be: EN(p) [EF1 [CF2 (Ott.)]–Steyn(p)]. Thus there is a partial coincidence of two of the three agents, while there are still three different identities at play.

In *g* the narrator is also an actor. After all, there is reference to discussions between the actor Steyn and the agent referring to itself as 'I.' The actor 'I,' which, from the point of view of identity, coincides with the narrator, is, however, probably – here again the fragment is too brief to give certitude – not an actant that is important from the point of view of action. It stands apart, observes the events, and relates the story according to its point of view. A narrator of this type is a *witness*. The question whether the story that it tells is invented can no longer be asked. The text is full of indications that the story must be considered true. Of course, this does not prove that it is also true; it merely speaks for the intentions of the narrator. The interpretation of this sentence is: (I narrate: (I declare as witness:)) Steyn's deep bass resounded in the vestibule. Since the narrator so clearly pretends to testify, it must also make clear how it got its information. In the first sentence of *g* it does so: its source, at that moment, is Steyn himself. With regard to the rest of the fragment we cannot tell. It may be that Ottilie has told the narrator this anecdote. If that is so, it will, no doubt, be indicated somewhere in the text. If not, it seems self-evident to presuppose that the narrator/character-witness was present at the scene. Let us suppose that this is the case. Then focalization is localized with the character-bound narrator who refers to itself and is, therefore, perceptible in the text. In that case the formula is: CN(p) [CF ('I')–Steyn(p)]. Now Ottilie has

disappeared as an agent, and both narration and focalization rest with
the CN(p).

In these examples we have seen four different narrative situations. In
d and *f* the narrator stood outside the fabula and in *e* and *g* it did not. In
d the focalizor was a character. In *f* we considered a case of embedded
focalization since here we saw an infiltration of external agents into
the *story*. In *e* the identification of the agents was closest: the narrator
and the focalizor were both the character Ottilie. In *g*, finally, narrator
and focalizor coincided; however, unlike *e*, not in the identity of one of
the active actors, but in the identity of a witness.

With these analyses, the fundamental distinction mentioned earlier
between a narrative 'I' that talks about itself and a narrative 'I' that
speaks of others has proven too gross. More distinctions between the
various 'I's are necessary. The narrative 'I' may exclusively relate, as in *d*;
it may also perceive, as in *e*, *f*, and *g*; and it may also act, as in *e* and *g*.
When it acts, this action may remain limited to *testimony*, as in *g*. The
traditional distinction between 'I'-narratives and 'he'-narratives is, as we
see, inadequate not only for terminological reasons. The difference
between *d* and *f* would remain inarticulate because the infiltration of
the 'I' into the *story* is neglected. The *narrative situations* analysed
here, that is the different relationships of the narrative 'I' to the object
of narration, may be constant within *one* narrative text. This means
that one can immediately, already on the first page, see which narrative
situation is being used. But it is an error to think that the narrative
situation cannot change. Displacements occur especially between *d*
and *f*. A narrator may remain imperceptible for a long time, but suddenly begin to refer to itself, sometimes in such a subtle manner that
the reader hardly notices.

However, in all cases focalization need not always remain with the
same agent. Technically it would be almost impossible to maintain
such continuity. A spectacular example of a novel in which focalization
rests from beginning to end with the CF, and narration with the EN(np),
is Alain Robbe-Grillet's *La Jalousie*. It is curious that precisely the consistency with which the technique is maintained has had the effect
that almost all critics have termed that anonymous agent a character: a
jealous husband. (Of course, the title has also been of influence in this.)

3   NON-NARRATIVE COMMENTS

The following excerpt from a randomly chosen children's book, *Danny*

Goes Shopping by L. Roggeveen, shows that the commentary of the external narrator may far exceed the function of *narrating*.

 1 Danny is barely able to hear him above the music.
 2 What is the matter? he thinks.
 3 Wide-eyed, he looks about him.
 4 Then he understands everything!
 5 There they come, arm in arm, with happy faces: Mr Alexander
 6 and Miss Ann!
 7 Mr Alexander is a poet. In his life, he has already written many
 8 rhymes. He has written a poem about Danny, one about
 9 currant bread; one about the singing of the nightingale in the
10 silent wood; and more than seven about Miss Ann!
11 Why did Miss Ann get so many poems?
12 Well, that is not difficult to guess!
13 Because Mr Alexander loves Miss Ann so much!
14 And, fortunately, Miss Ann loves Mr Alexander
15 just as much!
16 What do two people who love each other do?
17 Well, that also is not difficult to guess!
18 They get married! Of course! They did in the past,
19 they do so now, and they always will!
20 Mr Alexander and Miss Ann act just like all other people.
21 And today is *their* wedding day!
22 The mayor is waiting for the pair in the town hall.

Intuitively, we might summarize this page as follows: Danny watches the arrival of a bridal pair. Focusing on the actors and their actions, we would summarize: Danny sees, (the bridal pair arrives), the mayor is waiting. What do we say about those aspects of the text that disappear if we summarize in this manner? The answer to these questions will have to supply us with a criterion by which to distinguish between narrative and non-narrative parts of the text.

In lines 11 through 21 no events are presented. In addition, we are also not exclusively concerned with objects from the fabula. Summarizing lines 11 through 15, we may say that they convey: Mr Alexander and Miss Ann love each other. The two actants are described in their relationship to each other, or rather, the collective actant 'bridal pair' is described as consisting of two people who love each other. But in doing so, we neglect the word 'fortunately' in line 14. This word communicates an opinion. The opinion given here relates to the balance ('just as much') between the two actors. Apparently, a balance of this kind is evaluated favourably. This word cannot be termed descriptive, because it refers to something of a more general, more public and cultural bearing than the fabula. Parts of the text referring to something general we have termed *argumentative*. Argumentative textual passages do not refer to an element (process or object) of the fabula, but to an external topic. From this definition, it appears tha the term 'argumentative' should be taken in the widest sense. Not only opinions but also declarations with regard to the factual state of the world fall under this definition: for instance, sentences like 'water always boils at 100 degrees,' or 'Poland lies behind the Iron Curtain.' After all, sentences of this type also communicate no more than a *vision* of reality. High in the mountains, or using another method of scaling the thermometer, water would boil at a different 'temperature' (i.e. different representation of temperature). That the second example does not denote a fact but an opinion is evident when we change the sentences into 'Poland lies in Eastern Europe,' or 'Bonn lies behind the Iron Curtain.' Because the division between opinions and facts is so difficult to draw, we may consider 'argumentative' any statement that refers to something of general knowledge outside the fabula.

The word 'fortunately' formed part of a sentence that is, for the rest, descriptive. Analysing the story line by line, we may term lines 11–15 descriptive. Lines 16–19, however, do not contain any reference to elements of the story. Here we only see the representation of opinions about behaviour: people who love each other marry; this is what is usually done, and is as it should be. This opinion is represented in a certain form. This form, the game of question and answer in a mock dialogue, had already started in line 11. The form may have a convincing effect: the opinion is not presented as a personal one, but as something self-evident. This catechism is extended to convince the reader that s/he has known the truth all along. The exclamation marks and additions like 'of course' pursue the same goal.

In the next line, the actors are linked to the public opinion through mention of their conformism. They are merely described in that sentence. Only in the last sentence is a presentation of an event narrated. A new actor appears, the mayor. He is confronted with another actor, the bridal pair. Though the act of the mayor is durative, not circumscribed in time, it appears from the lines following those of our quoted passage that waiting must, nevertheless, be seen as an event. The

mayor gets angry because he has to wait, and takes action. It would be
naïve to suppose that only argumentative parts of the text communicate ideology. This may happen equally well in descriptive and narrative parts of the text; but the manner in which this happens is different.
In addition, the example shows that the discursive *form* – the catechis-
tic style here – itself has ideological implications. The argumentative
parts of the text often give *explicit* information about the ideology of a
text. It is, however, quite possible that such explicit statements are
treated ironically in other parts of the text, or are contradicted by
descriptive or narrative parts of the text to such an extent that the
reader must distance himself from them. If we want to evaluate the
ideological tenor of a text, an analysis of the relationship between
these three textual forms within the totality of the entire text may
help us.

4   DESCRIPTION

Delimitation

Lines 11-15 of the page from *Danny Goes Shopping* have been characterized as descriptive. Although descriptive passages would appear to
be of marginal importance in narrative texts, they are, in fact, both
practically and logically necessary. Narratology, therefore, must take
these segments of the text into account.

> *a* Bob Assingham was distinguished altogether by a leanness of per-
> son, a leanness quite distinct from physical laxity, which might
> have been determined, on the part of superior powers, by views of
> transport and accommodation, and which in fact verged on the
> abnormal.   (Henry James, *The Golden Bowl*)

The above excerpt presents no problems of classification. It is clearly a
description. Problems arise, however, as soon as one attempts to define
exactly what a description is. Is the following fragment, which not only
describes objects and people but also accounts for the passage of a certain stretch of time, descriptive?

> *b* Presently he told her the motion of the boat upon the stream was
> lulling him to rest. How green the banks were now, how bright the
> flowers growing on them, and how tall the rushes! Now the boat

was out at sea, but gliding smoothly on. And now there was a shore before him.   (Charles Dickens, *Dombey and Son*)

Intuitively speaking, we can say that this passage is a description. We will, therefore, define a description as a textual fragment in which features are attributed to objects. This aspect of attribution is the *descriptive function*. We will consider a fragment as descriptive when this function is dominant. Thus example *a* is dominantly descriptive, while *b* is a mixture of description and narration.

Within the realistic tradition, description has always been regarded as problematic.

In the *Republic*, Plato tried to rewrite fragments of Homer so that they would be 'truly' narrative. The first elements to be discarded were the descriptions. Even Homer himself attempted to avoid, or at least to disguise, descriptions by making them narrative. Achilles' shield is described as it is in the process of being made, Agamemnon's armour as he puts it on. In the nineteenth-century realistic novel, descriptions were at least motivated if they were not made narrative. And despite its efforts to avoid representation, the *nouveau roman* has continued to follow this tradition.

Motivation

Working from the premise that descriptions interrupt the line of the fabula, a typology has been constructed of the ways in which descriptions are inserted. Insertion necessitates *motivation*. If, as Zola argued, the novel should be objective, this notion of objectivity necessitates *naturalization* – that is, making those interruptions known as descriptions seem self-evident or necessary. This so-called objectivity is, in fact, a form of subjectivity when the meaning of the narrative resides in the reader's identification with the psychology of a character; this happens when characters are given the function of *authenticating* the narrative contents. If 'truth,' or even probability, is no longer a sufficient criterion to make narrative meaningful, only motivation can suggest probability, thus making the contents believable.

We can distinguish three types of motivation. Motivation is brought about by speaking, looking, or acting. The most effective, the most frequent, and the least noticeable form is motivation via looking. Motivation is, then, a function of focalization. A character sees an object. The description is the reproduction of what it sees. Looking at something requires time, and, in this fashion, the description is incorporated into the time lapse. But an act of looking must also have its motivation. There must be enough light so that the character is able to observe the object. There is a window, an open door, an angle of vision which also have to be described and therefore motivated. Further, the character must have both the time to look and a reason to look at an object. Hence the curious characters, the men of leisure, the unemployed, and the Sunday wanderers.

Given the fundamental arbitrariness of the elements of the fictional world, there is, equally fundamentally, no end to the need for motivation. The less obvious this motivation is, the more easily it can be terminated. In the following fragment, for example, the motivation is easily integrated into the description itself (italics mine):

> When they had washed they lay and *waited* again. There were fifteen beds in the tall, narrow room. The walls were painted grey. The windows were long but high up, *so that you could see only* the topmost branches of the trees in the grounds outside. Through *the glass* the sky had no colour.   (Jean Rhys, 'Outside the Machine,' *Tigers Are Better-Looking*)

The sentence immediately preceding the description ('they lay and waited again') gives sufficient motivation for the act of looking. Hospital patients, particularly after their morning wash, have an ocean of time ahead of them. Not only is the act of looking itself motivated, but also the contents of what the women see. And this is indicated by 'so that you could see,' by the boundaries of the area visible. The window motivates the fact that the women are able to see anything at all of what is happening outside the hospital. Also, the restricted quality of the field of vision is emphasized: 'Through the glass the sky had no colour.' This lack of colour has its own thematic meaning, so that even in this aspect the description is fully integrated into the text.

When a character not only looks but also describes what it sees, a certain shift in motivation occurs, although in principle all of the above-mentioned motivational demands remain valid. The act of speaking necessitates a listener. The speaker must possess knowledge which the listener does not have but would like to have. The listener can, for example, be blind, or young, or amateurish. There is yet a third form of motivation, which resembles Homeric description. The actor carries out an action with an object. The description is then made fully narrative. An example of this is the scene in Zola's *La Bête humaine* in which Jacques polishes (strokes) every individual component of his beloved locomotive.

Motivation occurs at the level of *text* when the character itself describes an object; at the level of *story* when the glance or vision of the character supplies the motivation; and at the level of *fabula* when the actor carries out an action with an object. One clear illustration of this last-mentioned form, and one which also demonstrates that a distinction between descriptive and narrative is no longer possible within this form, is the following 'description' of a dead man:

> Then they went into José Arcadio Buendia's room, shook him with all their might, screamed in his ear, and held a little mirror in front of his nose, but they weren't able to wake him.   (Gabriel García Márquez, *One Hundred Years of Solitude*)

Examples of the second type, motivation via focalization, are numerous. An illustration of the first type is the description of the Linton family as given by young Heathcliff in *Wuthering Heights*. He is forced to give this description because Nelly Dean has made him responsible for his escapades with Cathy and for the fact that he has returned alone.

Motivation is making the relationship between elements explicit. Precisely because these relationships are not self-evident in fictional texts, they can never be motivated enough. And, for this reason, motivation is, in the final analysis, arbitrary.

Types of Descriptions

Descriptions consist of a *theme* (e.g., 'house'), which is the object described, and a series of sub-themes (e.g., 'door,' 'roof,' 'room'), which are the components of the object. Taken together, the sub-themes constitute the *nomenclature*. They may or may not be accompanied by *predicates* (e.g., 'pretty,' 'green,' 'large'). These predicates are *qualifying* when they indicate a characteristic of the object ('pretty'); they are *functional* when they indicate a function, action, or possible use ('habitable for the six people'). Metaphors and comparisons can occur on any level. A metaphor can replace the theme or accompany it. The same holds for the sub-themes. The inclusive relation from theme to subtheme is synecdochical; the relation between the sub-themes is contiguous. Both relations can be termed *metonymical*. Between theme or sub-theme compared (the 'compareds' or c^d) and the predicates that replace them in metaphor, or specify them in comparison (the 'comparings' or c^i), the relation is termed *metaphorical*. On the basis of these two possible relations, we can roughly differentiate six types of description.

1   The Referential, Encyclopaedic Description
In principle, there are no figures of speech in this type of description. The selection of components is based upon the contiguity of the elements of the contents. This means that the presence of some elements implies the absence of others. The missing detail can be filled in by the reader. General characteristics imply specific characteristics, unless the latter represent the former. The objective is to convey knowledge. The encyclopedia is a model of this type of description.

2   The Referential-Rhetorical Description
The tourist guidebook rather than the encyclpaedia is the model for this second type of description. The units are now combined on the basis of both the contiguity of the components and their thematic function. The latter is evaluative. The objective is both to convey knowledge and to persuade. Persuasion occurs via the wording (a pleasing rhythm, a style that reflects the value of the object to be described, for example an 'expensive' style to describe the Champs-Elysées), and via the contents; persuasion also occurs via the choice of traditionally valued sub-themes, and by the addition of evaluative predicates. Even when a number of metaphors are included in such a description, the construction of the text continues to follow the principle of contiguity.

3   Metaphoric Metonymy
Here again, contiguity is the dominating principle of construction. But, in this case, metaphors are made of each individual component. Various compareds may, in fact, be omitted altogether. Only the comparings are found in the text which, as a result, is of very metaphoric nature. However, there is no relation of contiguity among the components of the c^i. Such a relation exists only among the implicit components of the c^d. Superficially, this type of description would make an incoherent impression upon the reader. That such is not the case indicates that the reader is engaged in a filling-in activity.

4   The Systematized Metaphor
This description is one large metaphor. The elements of the c^i and the

c^d are systematically related to one another. Each series is built upon the principle of contiguity. The series balance each other. The question as to which of the two series dominates the meaning cannot be answered without taking the context into consideration. Also included in this category are descriptions in which elements of the two series imply each other.

5   The Metonymic Metaphor
The description is one large metaphor. The elements are contiguously related to each other. They form a coherent description which, taken as a whole, is the c^i of a c^d. This relationship can remain implicit, in which case this type of description, when taken out of its context, cannot be distinguished from one of the other types. An explicit c^i results in a Homeric comparison.

6   The Series of Metaphors
This description consists of a metaphor which is expanded without continually referring to the c^d. The metaphor is repeatedly 'adjusted,' creating the impression that the c^d is elusive and indescribable.

5   LEVELS OF NARRATION

In the fragments *d* to *g* of our discussion of Couperus' *Of Old People* (p. 123) there was one phrase that remained unchanged throughout: 'Oh, that voice of Steyn's!' This phrase shows several characteristics of *emotive* language use – that is, the use of language which aims at self-expression of the speaker with regard to that about which it speaks. The element of this phrase that most strikingly indicates an emotive function is the word 'Oh.' The exclamation mark is a graphic representation of an emotionally laden intonation. Moreover, the grammatical peculiarity that this 'sentence' lacks a verb enforces its emotional effect.

Who is expressing this emotion? In other words, who says: 'mama Ottilie hissed'? The verb 'hiss' is in this sense a *declarative* verb, comparable to 'say.' Declarative verbs indicating that someone is about to speak are, in a narrative text, signs of a change of level in the narrative text. Another speaker enters the scene. In *d* the EN temporarily gives the word to Ottilie. The character Ottilie thus becomes a speaker at the second level, which we shall indicate with CN2. Note, however, that the use of CN2 is not entirely correct. Though Ottilie, at least temporarily, speaks, she does not *narrate*: what she says is not a story. Nevertheless, we shall use this indication because it makes clear that the character is a speaker, just like the narrator. What that narrator says is another matter, to which I shall return in the subsection *Relations between primary and embedded texts* later in this chapter. CN2, then, refers to a character that is given the word by the narrator of the first level, whether that is an EN1 or a CN1. CN2 is a speaker of the second level.

But what about that phrase in the fragments *e*, *f*, and *g*? It is on purpose that I have broken off the quotations in such a manner that we cannot see who speaks. The declarative verb is missing. In *e* there are two possibilities:

e.I   Oh, that voice of Steyn's, I hissed between my teeth.

e.II   Oh, that voice of Steyn's! I could not bear it any longer.

In *e.I* there is a declarative verb to indicate that what precedes is direct discourse, an embedded sentence. The speaker of the first level gives the word to the speaker of the second level. CN1 ('I') gives the word to CN2 ('I'). Just as in *d*, the emotive sentence is an *embedded sentence*, a sentence within a sentence, which we may represent with the use of brackets: CN1 [CN2]. The character is in both cases called Ottilie. But it is not the same Ottilie. CN1 only relates after the facts ('now') what CN2 said earlier ('then'). As a linguistic act, the emotive phrase forms part of the story. In a summary of the story, for instance, it might be represented thus: 'Ottilie expressed her irritation at the voice of Steyn.' Direct discourse or direct speech, an embedded sentence, is the object of a language act. Thus it is, in principle, an event like so many other events.

In *e.II* the emotive sentence belongs to the text of CN1. Though the *emotion* which is communicated does form part of the text, the expression of it does not. In a summary of the story we would read: 'Ottilie was irritated by Steyn's voice.' Not the act of verbal expression of the irritation but the irritation itself is, in principle, an event.

Fragment *f* contains the same possibilities:

f.I   Oh, that voice of Steyn's! Ottilie hissed between her teeth.

f.II Oh, that voice of Steyn's! I understood how Ottilie could not bear it any longer.

In f.I the EN1 gives the word to the CN2 (Ott.). Thus we have an ordinary embedded sentence, as we might find in any narrative text. The sequel given to the emotive phrase in f.II is of a piece with the interpretation of f given above, where we assumed that the EN(p) [EF] was on Ottilie's side. The words of the emotive phrase are thus ascribed to the EN(p), and the first level is maintained.

Still, something has changed in this fragment. Through the addition into the narrative text of a so clearly emotive sentence of the first level, the EN's voice becomes much more perceptible than it already was. It suggests in this emotive expression, that the EN has heard Steyn's voice, and that it has been irritated by it too. If it has heard the voice, it was, implicitly, present as an actor at the scene. That is why f and the variant f.II have the same structure as g. The narrative 'I' has become, by implication, a testifying actor. The reader will not be surprised therefore when a narrative situation with a CN-witness presents itself in the text. This is one of the cases in which a superficial, global characterization of the narrative situation may lead to mistakes. The EN1 may any minute start speaking on the second level as CN2, or do something else which makes it into an actor.

There is no reason to dwell on g. The possibilities are identical to those of f. Considering the narrative situation of g, it would seem obvious that either Ottilie speaks the emotive sentence as CN2, or the CN-witness speaks it as CN1.

In the subsection *The Focalized Object* in chapter 2, a distinction was made between perceptible and non-perceptible focalized objects. The same distinction must be made for the object of the narrative act. In the analysis of examples e through g, we only took into account the possibility that the character-speaker, the CN2, utters the words in fact. It does, however, also frequently occur that words, put in direct speech, are merely *thought*. Thus f might also have the following variant:

f.III Oh, that voice of Steyn's! Ottilie thought.

What the CN2 has narrated is not perceptible (np), because other actors, which may happen to be present, cannot hear the text. When an utterance which is narrated at the second level is not perceptible, this is also an *indication of fictionality*, an indication that the narrated story is invented. If the narrator wants to keep up the pretence that it relates true facts, it can never represent the thoughts of actors other than itself. This variant, then, only contradicts the pretence 'I state autobiographically' or, 'I testify' when a CN1 ('I') gives the word to a CN2 (another actor), while the verb is not declarative, but a synonym of 'to think.' Just as with focalization, this distinction is of importance in order to gain insight into the balance of powers between the characters. When a character does not hear what another character thinks, and readers do receive information concerning these thoughts, readers may easily come to expect too much of such a character. They may, for instance, expect that the character will take feelings, only formulated in thought, into account, in this case that Steyn will speak less loudly because his voice upsets Ottilie. But Steyn cannot know that it does, in this case, because he is outside the room; in another case, perhaps, because the irritation would not be expressed in words.

Intermediate Forms: Indirect Speech and Free Indirect Speech

Why does the way in which example f.II is phrased entail a change in narrative situation? Analysing the sentence, I have emphasized the signs of emotive function. I did this because, with this emotive function, the narrator refers to itself. If in a statement the feelings of the speaker are expressed, the statement *is about the speaker*. We might also say that such an expression is comparable to (I narrate:) I shall be twenty-one tomorrow, and not to (I narrate:) Elizabeth will be twenty-one tomorrow. Even if the narrator does not explicitly refer to itself, still, the 'I' narrates about itself. This means that an actor with the same identity as the narrator forms part of the fabula. Signs of emotive functioning are, therefore, also signs of self-reference. There are more signs of this kind. One may even speak of two different language situations: language about the contact between speaker and hearer, and language about others.

This distinction into two language situations, a personal and an impersonal one, may help us understand this and comparable phenomena. In f.II we have seen different pieces of evidence that the narrator is involved with its object. Its language is *personal* in that it refers to the position of the narrator itself. In doing so, it places itself on the same level as that about which it is speaking in the same statement. Thus it has made itself into a virtual (possible, still unrealized) actor. We may say that, in this case, narrative levels begin to intertwine. The impersonal language situation which we found in example *f*.II is invaded. The personal language situation intrudes, but not, as in *f*.I, on the second level. When an actor in a story begins to speak, it does so, in principle, in a personal language situation, in contact with another actor. In the basic narrative situation speech is only possible on one narrative level in the personal language situation. At first sight this happens when the narrator addresses itself explicitly, or implicitly, to the reader; at the second level, when an actor speaks to another actor (this may be the speaking actor itself). In *f*.II we find a 'mixture' of the two narrative levels, which we may call *text interference*.

The two narrative situations are to be distinguished on the basis of *references* in the text to personal or impersonal language situations. These references are to be taken as signals, as signs indicating: 'this is a(n) (im)personal language situation.' These signals may be related to the following forms:

		personal	*impersonal*
1	personal pronouns	I/you	he/she
2	grammatical person	first and second person	third person
3	tense	not all past tenses are possible	all past tenses
4	*deixis*: indicative pronouns	this, these	that/those
	adverbs of place	here/there	in that place
	adverbs of time	today, tomorrow	that day, the day after
5	emotive words and aspects	Oh!	(absent)
6	conative words and aspects: address, command, question	please	(absent)
7	modal verbs and adverbs which indicate uncertainty in the speaker	perhaps	(absent)

When the signals of the personal language situation refer to the language situation of the narrator, we are dealing with a perceptible narrator (N1(p)). When the signals refer to the language situation of the actors, and a clear change of level has been indicated by means of a declarative verb, a colon, quotation marks, etc., we speak of a personal language situation at the second level. (CN2). This situation may be called *dramatic*: just as on the stage, actors communicate through speech in a personal language situation. When, however, the signals refer to a personal language situation in which the actors participate without previously stepping down from their narrative level, then we have *text interference*. This was the case in *f.*II. The N1(p) stepped across, so to say, to the second level. But that was just one possibility. The inverse occurs more often. Then the *words* of the actors are represented at the first level, so that the narrator adopts the actor's discourse.

The most common form of this is *indirect discourse*. Here the narrator represents the words of the actor as it is supposed to have uttered them. Compare the following examples:

h Elizabeth said: 'I think I shall be able to find time to go out with you tomorrow night.'

i Elizabeth said that she might be able to find time to go out with him tomorrow night.

j Elizabeth said that she would probably have time to go out with him tomorrow night.

k Elizabeth said that she would probably have time to go out with him the following night.

In *i*, *j*, and *k* the contents of Elizabeth's words are represented in an equally adequate manner. The words themselves are represented with maximum accuracy in *i*, with less accuracy in *j*, and still less in *k*. *It is impossible and irrelevant to reconstruct the 'original' direct speech from indirect discourse.* Comparing the examples, however, we may say that *i* represents more accurately than *j*, and *j* than *k*. We do not need *h* to come to this conclusion. In *i* we read 'she might be able to,' where the modal indication of uncertainty 'might' has been combined with a subject-oriented positive verb, 'be able to find.' 'Tomorrow' is a deictic adverb of time. In *j* the modal form is still present, but less strongly, in 'would probably.' The adverb is less emphatic about personal uncertainty than the expression 'might be able.' In *j* we also find the deictic adverb 'tomorrow night.' In *k* only the weak modal value of 'probably' is a trace of the personal language situation. In *i*, *j*, and *k*, we find, compared to *h*, a number of signs of the impersonal language situation, because the sentence is in indirect discourse. The personal pronoun 'I' has been changed into 'she'; the verb is now in the third person, and not in the first; and the present future has been changed into a past future. On the basis of this analysis, we may name three characteristics which distinguish these forms.

1 Indirect discourse is narrated at a higher level than the level at which the words in the fabula are supposed to have been spoken.
2 The narrator's text explicitly indicates that the words of an actor are narrated by means of a declarative verb and a conjunction, or a substitute for it.
3 The words of the actor appear to have been rendered with maximum precision and elaboration.

The first characteristic distinguishes indirect discourse from direct discourse. The second characteristic distinguishes indirect discourse from a mode of representation which is even more indirect: *free indirect discourse*. The third characteristic distinguishes (free) indirect discourse from narrator's text. This last distinction is the one that gives us most problems. That is because the third characteristic is relative.

When characteristic 2 of indirect discourse is left out, and characteristic 3 is present, we have free indirect discourse. Then we have a form of interference between narrator's text and actor's text. Signals of the personal language situation of the actor and of the (im)personal language situation of the narrator cross, without explicit reference to this. Thus we have:

1 Elizabeth might be able to go out with him tomorrow.

'Tomorrow' and 'might' indicate the personal language situation of the actor Elizabeth, while the other signals suggest the impersonal language situation: third person, past tense.

Precisely because the second characteristic of indirect discourse is lacking – the explicit sign that there is indirect discourse – we cannot always be sure whether we have to do with indirect discourse or ordinary, 'pure' narrator's text. After all, the third characteristic is relative. That is why we only distinguish free indirect discourse from the narrator's text when there are positive indications that there is indeed representation of *words of an actor*. Such indications are:

1 The above-mentioned signals of a personal language situation, referring to an actor.
2 A strikingly personal style, referring to an actor.
3 More details about what has been said than is necessary for the course of the fabula.

To demonstrate this I shall represent one event – Elizabeth seeks a confrontation with John – in various forms.

direct speech	*m*	Elizabeth said: 'I refuse to go on living like this.'
indirect speech	*n*. I	Elizabeth said that she refused to go on living like that.
	n. II	Elizabeth said that she would not go on living like that.
free indirect discourse	*o*. I	Elizabeth would be damned if she'd go on living like this.
	o. II	Elizabeth would not go on living like this.
narrator's text	*p*. I	Elizabeth did not want to go on living in the manner disclosed.
	p. II	Elizabeth stopped.

In the analysis of these sentences I assume that the verb 'to refuse' fits the usage of the actor Elizabeth, and not the narrator. Of course, without a context, such an assumption is not warranted.

The direct discourse in *m* should not give any problems. We read the precise text uttered by the actor, and the indications of the changes in level are explicit. As soon as the actor's text is given by the narrator in the following sentences, changes occur. In *n*.I, the actor's text is represented as exactly as possible. As far as contents are concerned, this is also true for *n*.II. But the style which – we may assume – is clearly recognizable as the personal style of the irritated actor refers to a personal language situation of the actor, probably a quarrel. The difference between *n*.I and *n*.II on the one hand, and *o*.I and *o*.II on the other, lies in the presence or absence of a declarative verb with a conjunction. In *o*.II the actor's text has been represented with less exactitude than in *o*.I. Of course, in studying narrative texts, we never have such comparable

combinations at hand. But even without comparison, we may say that
o.I is strongly coloured by the actor's text, and o.II by the narrator's text.
Still we also detect free indirect discourse in o.II, because the adjunct
'like this' betrays a personal language situation of the actor. The presence of these words also distinguishes o.II from p.I. In p.I I have used the
rather heavy-handed expression 'in the manner disclosed' in order to
avoid a deictic element. But even if I had chosen 'in that manner,' 'that'
would refer to what had been stated earlier, hence to the language
situation of the narrator, and not the actor. In p.I and II we have a narrator's text. We cannot distinguish any signal of the actor's personal language situation. We have no reason to take p.I as the representation of
certain spoken words. Finally, p.II is the purest form of the narrator's
text. The content is presented as an act, a verbal act of the actor. The
words in which the refusal is uttered are not mentioned at all.

Indirect discourse, free indirect discourse, and the narrator's text in
which language acts are narrated are all three forms in which the words
of an actor are narrated at first level. The degree to which, in this series,
justice is done to the *text* of the actor decreases; on the other hand, the
degree to which the speaking of the actor is seen as an act gradually
increases. The interference of narrator's text and actor's text may, therefore, occur in widely varying proportions. At the first level, the actor's
text is given minimal reflection in indirect discourse, but even here
variations are possible. In free indirect discourse, sometimes the narrator's text dominates (o.II), then again the actor's text (o.I). In the narrator's text the words of the actor are not represented as *text*, but as an
act. In that case we no longer speak of text interference.

Relations between Primary and Embedded Texts

When there is text interference, narrator's text and actor's text are so
closely related that a distinction into narative levels can no longer be
made. The relationship between the narrative levels has exceeded the
boundary of maximum intensity. When the texts do not interfere, but
are clearly separate, there may still be a difference in the degree to
which the embedded actor's text and the primary narrator's text are
related. In this paragraph, I shall discuss a number of possible relationships between texts. We shall always term the narrator's text 'primary,'
without implying a value-judgment. It only means that the connection
is hierarchical, in the technical sense. Eventually, the narrative text
constitutes a whole, into which, from the narrator's text, other texts

may be *embedded*. The dependence of the actor's text with regard to the narrator's text should be seen as the dependence of a subordinate clause to a main clause. According to this principle, narrator's text and actor's text are not of equal status. The hierarchical position of the texts is indicated by the fundamental principle of *level*. The relations between narrator's text and actor's text may be of difference in kind and intensity. Quantitative aspect is of influence here: the more sentences frame the actor's text, the stronger is the dependence.

Embedded Narrative Texts

A first difference resides in the nature of the embedded text. This can be investigated with the same criteria which have been given in the introduction for the relative definition of a corpus. When these criteria for narrativity have been met, the embedded text may also be considered as a narrative text. This is most obvious in so-called *frame narratives*: narrative texts in which at second or third level a complete story is told. The classic example is the story cycle of the *Arabian Nights*. Here we find narration at several levels. The primary narrative presents the story of Scheherazade, threatened with death by her husband, the king. Only if she succeeds in fascinating him with her stories will she survive the night, night after night. Every night she tells a story; in that story new stories are embedded, so that we have the construction: Scheherazade tells A that B tells that C tells, etc., sometimes until the eighth degree.

Relations between Primary Fabula and Embedded Text

When the embedded text presents a complete story with an elaborate fabula, we gradually forget the fabula of the primary narrative. In the case of the *Arabian Nights*, this forgetting is a sign that Scheherazade's intention has succeeded. As long as we forget that her life is at stake, the king will too, and that was her purpose. In that case, the apparently loose relationship between primary and embedded text is relevant to the development of the primary fabula. The *narrative act* of the actor Scheherazade which produces the embedded text is an important *event* – even *the* event – in the fabula of the primary text. The relationship between the primary text and the narrative subject lies in the relationship between the primary *fabula* and the embedded *narrative* act. Summarizing the primary fabula we might also say: 'That night Scheherazade enchanted the king.' From this summary it is immediately clear what the symbolic function of the act of narration is. That interpretation is endorsed by the motif for the threat: the infidelity of a previous wife of the king. To the king and to Scheherazade narrating means *life*, in two different senses.

Relations between Primary Fabula and Embedded Fabula

Another possible relationship between the two texts presents itself when the two fabulas are related to each other. Then there are two possibilities. The embedded story can *explain* the primary story, or it may *resemble* the primary story. In the first case the relationship is made explicit by the actor narrating the embedded story; in the second the explanation is usually left to the reader, or merely hinted at, in the fabula.

The Embedded Fabula Explains the Primary Fabula
In that case it depends on the relationship between the two which fabula will be seen as more important by the reader. It may very well be the embedded one. Often the primary fabula is hardly more than the occasion for a perceptible, character-bound narrator to narrate a story. The primary fabula may, for instance, be presented as a situation in which the necessary change cannot be made, because ... Then the embedded narrative follows. A stereotypical example: a boy asks a girl to marry him. She loves him, and would rise on the social scale by marrying him. Still she cannot accept him. The reason is [that in the past, she has been seduced by a ruthless villain with the usual consequences. Since that time she carries the stain of her contact with a perfidious man who took advantage of her innocence. He seduced her in the following manner ...]. The girl retires to a nunnery, and the boy soon forgets her.

The Embedded Fabula Explains and Determines the Primary Fabula
The embedded text may take up the larger part of a book, as sometimes happens in cautionary tales of this type. The primary fabula is minimal here, because the number of the events is small: proposal – exposition – rejection. In the above example, the embedded story explains the primary fabula. The relationship between the fabulas was merely explanatory. The situation was unchangeable. The fact that the woman tells her story is of no influence on the outcome of the primary fabula. In other cases, however, an explanation of the starting situation may also

lead to change. For instance, if the young man had been very moved by the sad account of his beloved's past, and recognized her innocence, he might have come to the conclusion that he wished to forget the past. Thus he would 'give her a second chance.' The function of the embedded fabula is then no longer merely explanatory. The exposition influences the primary fabula.

In proportion to the degree of intrinsic interest of the fabula in the primary, as well as in the embedded, text, the tie between the two texts will be more intense, and the explanation more functional. The previous, fictitious example is extreme in one respect, *Of Old People* in another. Here, the embedded texts relate bit by bit the story of the events in the Indies, which explain a number of events in the primary fabula. In this case, the relationship between the texts is so intense because the embedded fabula, the 'Thing,' the murder in the Indies, is always presented only in part. Moreover, the functioning of the CN2 (Harold) is also curious. Sometimes he narrates the story of CN2 (Harold), the older man who remembers things, then again he tells the story of CN3 (Little Harold), the boy who witnessed without understanding. Views of the past as seen then are presented, intermingled with images of the past interpreted with the insight of the present. Within this subtext, a double, or subtly varying, focalization is narrated. This, in turn, relates to the events in the primary fabula, the slow, inevitable encroachment of the past upon the present. The influence of the explanatory sub-fabula, in all its doubleness, is of decisive importance.

When the embedded text is, however, restricted to a minimum, the importance for the primary story diminishes. A sentence like 'I shall kill you at dawn to prevent you from deceiving me, *because my first wife betrayed me*' (*Arabian Nights*) contains an example of a minimal, declarative, embedded narrative text.

The Fabulas Resemble One Another

The fabulas 'resemble one another.' If they resembled each other completely, we would have two identical texts. In that case, the primary text would cite itself. Resemblance, however, can never be absolute. Therefore, we speak of stronger and weaker resemblance. Even in passport photographs, taken with the express intention to show resemblance to the person portrayed, there may be different degrees of likeness. When can we speak of resemblance between two different fabulas? A simple and relative solution to such a problem is this: we speak of resemblance when two fabulas can be paraphrased in such a way that the summaries have one or more striking elements in common. The degree of resemblance is determined by the number of terms the summaries share. An embedded text that presents a story which, according to this criterion, resembles the primary fabula may be taken as a sign of the primary fabula.

This phenomenon is comparable to infinite regress. In French the term is *mise en abyme*. This term derives from heraldry, where the phenomenon occurs in pictorial representation. We, however, have to do with infinite regress in the medium of language. It would be wrong, therefore, to overstress the analogy to graphic representation, since in language *mise en abyme* occurs in a less 'ideal' form. What is put into the perspective of infinite regress is not the totality of an image, but only a part of the text, or a *certain aspect*. To avoid needless complications, I suggest we use the term *mirror-text* for *mise en abyme*.

An Indication to the Reader

When the primary fabula and the embedded fabula can be paraphrased in such a manner that both paraphrases have one or more elements in common, the subtext is a *sign* of the primary text. The place of the embedded text – the mirror-text – in the primary text determines its function for the reader. When the mirror-text occurs near the beginning the reader may, on the basis of the mirror-text, predict the end of the primary fabula. In order to maintain suspense, the resemblance is often veiled. The embedded text will only be interpreted as mirror-text, and 'give away' the outcome, when the reader is able to capture the partial resemblance through abstraction. That abstract resemblance, however, is usually only captured after the end, when we know the outcome. Thus suspense is maintained, but the prefiguring effect of the mirror-text is lost.

Another possibility is the inverse: the fabula of the embedded text does not veil its resemblance with the primary fabula. The foreshadowing effect is preserved at the expense of suspense. This does not always imply that suspense is entirely lost. Another kind of suspense may arise. From the kind in which both reader and character are equally in the dark, we have stepped up to a second kind: the reader knows, but the character does not, how the fabula will end. The question that the reader raises at the end is not 'How does it end?' but 'Will the character discover in time?' We can never be sure of this, because resemblance is never perfect. It may happen that the embedded fabula resembles the primary one *apart from the ending*.

When a mirror-text has been added more towards the end of the primary text, the problem of suspense presents itself less emphatically. The course of the fabula is then largely familiar, the function of the mirror-text is no longer predictive, but retrospective. A simple repetition of the primary fabula in a mirror-text would not be as interesting. Its function is mostly *significance enhancing*. The paraphrase of the primary and of the embedded text that we have made in order to infer resemblance will have a more general significance. This more general sense – a human being always loses against a bureaucracy, or, even more abstractly, 'no one escapes fate,' lifts the whole narration on to another level. Kafka's novels do this. The mirror-text serves as directions for use: the embedded story contains a suggestion how the text should be read. Even in this case, the embedded text functions as a sign to the reader.

An Indication to the Actor

Just now I have hinted at the possibility that the actor itself may also interpret the mirror-text as a sign. In this way it may find out the course of the fabula in which it is itself engaged. Thus it may influence the fabula's outcome. It can take fate into its own hands. This happens, for instance, in Poe's 'The Fall of the House of Usher.' The actor who relates the story in which he himself figures saves his life through the correct interpretation of the signs that are presented to him. In the embedded text, which is read out loud, there is mention of a fall. This word 'fall' and the concept 'house' have two meanings. Fall refers of course to the reduction of a house to ruins, but also to the end of a family line. The Usher family will fall with the death of its last descendant, and the castle will fall down. This is what the CN ('I'-witness) realizes. Because he has the insight that double meanings should be taken seriously, the actor is able to interpret the embedded fabula as a mirror of what is to happen. That is why he can save himself. He flees, and behind him he sees the castle fall down. Thus he can be a witness and relate this curious story.

This mirror-text is interesting for yet other reasons. The actor's realization that double meanings should be taken seriously is itself a sign. It is a 'prescription' for the reading of literature. The embedded text, which is double in meaning, consists of a piece of literature. This text,

interpreted in the widest sense, suggests: 'Literature has a double meaning, or it is not literature.' Thus this embedded text also implies a
poetics, a declaration of principle with regard to the ideas about literature that have been embodied in the events in this text. Just as for the
actor-witness the right interpretation of the doubleness of the meaning
of the embedded text was a matter of life or death, so the double interpretation of the relationship between primary and embedded text is a
matter of life and death, to be or not to be, for literature. As is so often
the case, the title of the text, through its use of puns, has already given
an indication of these meanings. But, at the same time, this title seems
deceptively simple. It needs the whole story to disclose the doubleness
of its meaning.

Non-narrative Embedded Texts

By far the majority of embedded texts are non-narrative. No story is
related in them. The content of an embedded text may be anything:
assertions about things in general, discussions between actors, descriptions, confidences, etc. The most predominant form is the *dialogue*.
Dialogues between two or more actors may even make up the larger
part of the entire text. Dialogue is a form in which the actors themselves, and not the primary narrator, utter language. The total of the
sentences spoken by the actors produces meaning in those parts of the
text. Such embedded texts share that characteristic with dramatic
texts. In dramatic texts the whole text consists of the utterances of
actors who together, in their interaction, produce meaning. (Except, of
course, the stage directions in the paratext, but this is another problem.) The dialogues embedded in a narrative text are dramatic in kind.
The more dialogue a narrative text contains, the more dramatic that
text is. Hence the relative nature of the definition of a corpus. Of
course, the same applies to other genres: in a dramatic text we may
have a narrator, as happens often in the plays of Bertold Brecht. The
statement 'The more dialogue, the more drama,' however, is a simplifi-
cation, since not only quantity is of importance here. The 'purity' of the
dialogues also influences the degree to which a text may be experienced as dramatic. When between each utterance of an actor the
primary narrator intervenes with additions like 'Elizabeth said,' or even
more elaborate commentary, the hierarchical relationship between N1
and N2 remains clearly visible. When the clauses follow each other

without intervention by the N1, we are likely to forget that we are dealing with an embedded dialogue.

When the embedded text is spoken – or 'thought' – by one actor, it is
a soliloquy or monologue. The content of a monologue may, again, be
practically anything. There is no intrinsic difference between an
embedded monologue and other language use. It may contain confidences, descriptions, reflections, self-reflection, whatever one wishes.
This is the reason we will not discuss the monologue further here. It
would need a complete text theory to discuss all kinds of embedded
texts. For dramatic embedded texts, one should consult the theory of
drama. For some embedded monologues one might consult a theory of
poetry. Therefore, I shall be brief about the relationship between the
primary text and the embedded non-narrative one. When the embedded
text itself is not discussed in greater detail, little can be said about its
relationship to the primary one. In every case, the relationship may be
determined by two factors. Explicit commentary on the embedded text
which influences our reading of that text may be given by the N1. That
commentary may be disguised when the embedded text is only hinted
at by implication. Also, the relationship between the two contents
determines the relationship. The contents of the embedded text sometimes link with that of the primary one, sometimes it is even its natural
sequel. It is perhaps completely divorced; or it has an explanatory function; it is similar to the primary text; it contradicts or contravenes it. In
each case, the relationship is different. It is, therefore, impossible to
just suppose that, as a general rule, the assertions of an actor carry the
meaning of the whole text. In face of the hierarchical relation between
the two texts, one negative word of the N1 would, in principle, be sufficient to radically change the meaning of the whole.

6   REMARKS AND SOURCES

I have limited myself in the choice of topics for this chapter. Only the
status of the narrative agent and its relationship to what is narrated
have been discussed. This restriction is the effect of the decision,
already put forth in the introduction, to limit our subject matter. Narratology studies narrative texts only in so far as they are narrative; in
other words, in their narrativity. In particular, the topic of the third
chapter, the text, might also be studied in several other aspects. Linguistically oriented disciplines such as stylistics, but also grammar,

syntax, and semantics are necessary in a complete investigation of the text, but have been left out deliberately here. Side trips to other disciplines would inevitably have interfered with the systematic organization of this study.

Nevertheless, the connections with related disciplines have made themselves felt at several points. The distinction between direct, indirect, and free indirect discourse, which I have discussed here because it concerns the status of the narrative agent with regard to the object of narration, is one of the classic topics of linguistics. Thus the delimitation of the subject of discussion, however strictly envisaged, will never be more than preliminary.

The concept of the *implied author* has been introduced by Booth (1961). The confusion between pragmatics and semantics that has arisen around this concept is especially noticeable in the work of Booth's followers, who are numerous. A clear discussion of this problem can be found in Pelc (1971).

Benveniste (1966) made the distinction between personal and impersonal use of language, for which he used the terms 'histoire' and 'discours.' Because these terms have given rise to confusion, I have avoided them there.

On text interference, see Doležel (1973).

About the difference between 'pure' narration and non-narrative commentary, see Genette (1969), which has appeared in English as 'Boundaries of Narrative.' There are many different views of free indirect discourse. A clear survey is offered by McHale (1978). Less systematic is Lanser (1982). A promising theory is that of Banfield (1982). Perry (1979) labels the phenomenon 'combined discourse.'

Dällenbach (1977) wrote an interesting book about mirror-texts. A critical discussion and systematization is offered by Bal (1985). See also Jefferson (1983).

There is a lengthy article (1972) and a book (1981) by Hamon about description. The typology of motivation is based on this article. The six types of description are largely inspired by Lodge (1977). The concept of authentication is discussed in a very useful article by Doležel (1980).

For Those Who Wish To Know More

Structuralism
The models that derive from structuralism have been critically dis-

cussed by Culler (1975) in a clear survey. In a later book (1983), the biases of structuralism are discussed from a still more critical point of view.

Barthes and Greimas
One of the many critical applications of the analytical model of Barthes is Chatman (1969). A simple introduction to Greimas' work does not exist. Courtés' attempt (1976) is not very successful; it does not help in understanding Greimas' theory. It is easier, in fact, to read Greimas' own applications, such as the analysis of a short story by De Maupassant (1976). Though this is not easy to understand, it gives insight into the possibilities of the theory, which is more comprehensive than the actantial model referred to in this text. Greimas and Courtés (1979) present the theory in a dictionary form.

Genette
The work of Genette has often been discussed; the best discussion is that of Rimmon (1976). She places the theory in the development of structuralism, and also surveys consistency and practical usefulness. Culler's preface to the English edition is a short and clear introduction to all of Genette's work.

Characters
There is little systematic discussion on character apart from the actantial model. The most useful article is that by Hamon (1977). See also his book of 1983. A historical survey of the character in the Aristotelian tradition is offered by Walcutt (1966). Like Harvey (1965), he does not go beyond Forster's distinction (1927). Chatman (1972) does criticize the central role of the action in structuralist theories of the character, but he does not offer a viable substitute. Rimmon-Kenan (1983) presents work on character by the Tel Aviv school, among others' Hrushovski's.

Descriptions
Here too, Hamon's contribution is the most systematic one apart from the many analyses of descriptions in which its symbolic importance was especially stressed. A special number of *Yale French Studies* provides interesting suggestions (Kittay 1981). A survey of the problems is to be found in Bal (1982). About the difference between narrative and non-narrative (descriptive and argumentative) parts of the text, see Genette (1969).

Free Indirect Discourse and Personal Language Use
In addition to the work of Banfield mentioned above, see McHale
(1978), which discusses the most important suggestions. Doležel (1973)
defends the opinion that free indirect discourse is a form of 'text interference.' Ron (1981) discusses it from the point of view of 'deconstruction.' Tamir (1978) discusses several forms of personal narrative from a
linguistic point of view.

Focalization
Several publications by Perry (e.g. 1979) consider the problem of 'perspective' in an original manner. Doležel (1980) links it to the problem of
authentication, the credibility of various sources of information in a
fictional text. In this article, he also broaches the subject of the usefulness of so-called 'possible world semantics' for the theory of literature.

Dialogues
Glowiński (1974) discusses the status of dialogues. In comparison with
Pelc (1971) his opinions have been given less theoretical underpinning,
but he provides more possibilities for the analysis of the text. The two
articles could be combined fruitfully. Bal (1981) discusses dialogue as
an embedded part of texts. For other aspects, see the theory of drama.
Platz-Waury (1978) is a simple introduction; Van Kesteren and Schmid
(1975) contains a number of important articles. A second collection is
in preparation. Segre (1980) is also useful.

The Audience and the Reader
Recently, attention has been paid to the narratee. See the articles by
Prince (e.g. 1973). The publications of Iser (e.g. 1978) focus on the
reader. Eco (1976, 1979) discusses the reader's activity in building a
fictional world while decoding a text. Pratt also discusses a similar
problem (1977).

Periodicals and Serial Publications
For those who want to keep informed of the latest developments in
narratology, it is advisable to consult the following periodicals regularly. *PTL, A Journal for Descriptive Poetics and Theory of Literature*
used to be edited by B. Hrushovski of the Institute for Poetics and
Semiotics at Tel-Aviv. It appeared from 1976 to 1979. During these
three years it published an unusually great number of important articles. It has now been replaced with the equally valuable *Poetics Today*.

Since 1970 we have had the French periodical *Poétique*. Until recently it was under the general editorship of Genette and Todorov. Also important is *Littérature*. In English there is the crucial journal *New Literary History*, edited by Ralph Cohen; also *Semiotica*, *Critical Inquiry*, and *Diacritics*, and in England the *Journal of Literary Semantics*. A series of introductory books has appeared with Methuen under the general editorship of Terence Hawkes. They are unequal in quality, but contain a number of good clear introductions, e.g. Roger Fowler on stylistics, and Rimmon-Kenan on narratology.

It would be excellent if there were a periodical devoted exclusively to the teaching of literature.

Appendix on Quoted Dutch Novelists

J.M.A. Biesheuvel (b. 1939) comes from a Protestant Christian background. He alternately studied law and worked as a sailor. He is a full-time writer now, performing on TV and giving lectures. In his work, which is partly autobiographical, he plays on his experience as a patient in a psychiatric hospital. Biesheuvel is considered a post-modern writer, of a typically Dutch kind, where intense story-telling, often taking the form of gossip, is thematized. In his plea for the absurdity of human behaviour, of human life, existentialism persists. *De weg naar het licht* (The Way to the Light) appeared in 1977, from Meulenhoff of Amsterdam. The quotation is from the short story 'Faust,' a parodic variation on the Faust motif, full of crazy fantasies caused by psychiatric medication.

Louis Couperus (1863–1923) grew up as one of many children in a family of colonial administrators. His father was severe and demanding, and the child was bound to disappoint him. The family spent several years in the Indies. His many works include psychological novels, symbolic fairy tales, mythological novels, historical novels, often set in a decadent society, short stories, travel accounts, and journalism. His recurrent theme is the predominance of fate in human life. Fate, in Couperus' view, is an almost personified, basically obscure force, impregnated with guilt. The opposition between the north, as cold, somber, male, and bourgeois, and south, as sensual and female, structures many of his novels.

   Of Old People, and Things That Pass (1906) can be considered a typically Dutch variant of Naturalism: hereditary flaws persevere through three generations, guilt is connected with passion and violence is staged in both the Indies and The Hague. The 'old people' are more and more haunted by the murder of the old woman's husband they accomplished sixty years ago in the Indies, while the secret, after all these years, becomes more and more in danger of revelation.

Harry Mulisch (b. 1927) lived with his German-Austrian father after the divorce of his parents. His mother was Jewish. The war influenced him deeply. Mulisch's philosophy has been elaborated in his entire oeuvre, and recently explicitly in his *De compositie van de wereld* (The Composition of the World), 1980. For him, art is the only possible way of understanding and knowing the world. Reality only becomes meaningful when it is recreated in art. Language disposes of a magical power that allows the writer to create and to conquer time. Mulisch considers the mystical philosopher Pythagoras to be the first exemplary artist. The collection of short stories *What Happened to Sergeant Massuro?*, published in 1972, contains the story with the same title, which was written in 1955. The story consists of a report, written by Massuro's friend, on behalf of the ministry of war, in which the friend tries to explain, or rather to understand, the mysterious event that happened to Massuro: his slow petrification during an expedition in the jungle of New Guinea. The personal language-situation is relevant for the understanding of the story, which, in its dense symbolic structure, is reminiscent of *Heart of Darkness*.

Gerard Reve (b. 1923) claims to have inherited his verbal talent from his father, a communist journalist, and his romantic feelings from his mother. During the first period of his authorship (1946–56) he wrote realistic symbolic novels, set in a lower-class milieu, often featuring young boys or adolescents. *De avonden* dates from this period (1947). The (anti-)hero of this novel fills up the boredom of his daily life with counting the hours and sharply observing others, his parents and his friends. Reality is presented as a meaningless sequence of details without connections. The novel presents the ten days of the Christmas period in 1946. Nothing happens. Later, the author becomes *the* writer of romantic-ironic feelings, and the works of his later period often take the epistolary form. His ostentatious stance for homosexuality, (iconoclastic) Catholicism, and reactionary political views, including racism, made him the constant centre of public attention and the source of many controversies. His irony makes his position disturbingly unclear. He doubtless contributed importantly to the emancipation of homosexuality in the Netherlands.

Jan Wolkers (b. 1925) was the third son of an orthodox Christian family with a dominant father. Although a relatively successful sculptor, he is famous as a novelist and writer of short stories. His early work settles accounts with his Calvinist background, as exemplified by his *Terug naar Oegstgeest* (Return to Oegstgeest) of 1965. The uncensored representation of sexuality and sadism, in an atmosphere of guilt and penance, made Wolkers very popular among the young. His later work evolves towards a preoccupation with decay. The best-known novel of this period, *Turks fruit* (Turkish Delight), is internationally known. *De kus* (The Kiss) is the report of a tour through Indonesia, paralleled by a gradual questioning of masculine values and strength. The description of the roof of the Burrubudur temple marks the beginning of physical decay which befalls the I-character's 'superman'-friend. Wolkers is the most popular Dutch writer; significantly, his work has never been seriously studied.

Bibliography

Bachelard, Gaston
- 1957. *La Poétique de l'espace*. Paris: Presses universitaires de France
Bal, Mieke
- 1978. 'Mise en abyme et inconicité.' *Littérature* 29, 116–28
- 1981. 'Notes on Narrative Embedding.' *Poetics Today* 2:2
- 1982. 'On the Meaning of Descriptions.' Twentieth Century Literature
  (special issue on the Structural Analysis of Meaning, ed. Nomi Tamir-Ghez)
- 1984. *Narratologie. Essais sur la signification narrative dans quatre romans
  modernes*. Utrecht: Hes
- 1985. *Femmes imaginaires. L'ancien testament au risque d'une narratologie
  critique*. Utrecht: Hes; Montréal: HMH
Banfield, Ann
- 1982. *Unspeakable Sentences*. London: RKP
Barthes, Roland
- 1977. 'Introduction to the Structural Analysis of Narratives.' *Image-Music-
  Text*. London: Fontana
Benveniste, Emile
- 1970. *Problems in General Linguistics*. Coral Gables: University of Miami
  Press
Booth, Wayne C.
- 1961. *The Rhetoric of Fiction*. Chicago: University of Chicago Press
Bremond, Claude
- 1973. *Logique du récit*. Paris: Seuil
Chatman, Seymour
- 1969. 'New Ways of Analysing Narrative Structures, with an Example from

Joyce's *Dubliners.' Language and Style* 2, 3–36
- 1972. 'On the Formalist-Structuralist Theory of Character.' *Journal of Literary Semantics* 1, 57–79
- 1978. *Story and Discourse*. Ithaca: Cornell University Press
Courtés, J.
- 1976. *Introduction à la sémiotique narrative et discursive*. Paris: Hachette
Culler, Jonathan
- 1975. *Structuralist Poetics, Structuralism, Linguistics and the Study of Literature*. London: RKP
- 1983. *On Deconstruction*. London: RKP
Dällenbach, Lucien
- 1977. *Le récit spéculaire: Essai sur la mise en abyme*. Paris: Seuil
Doležel, Lubomír
- 1973. *Narrative Modes in Czech Literature*. Toronto: University of Toronto Press
- 1980. 'Truth and Authenticity in Narrative.' *Poetics Today* 1:3, 7–25
Eco, Umberto
- 1976. *A Theory of Semiotics*. Bloomington: Indiana University Press
- 1979. *The Role of the Reader*. Bloomington: Indiana University Press
Forster, E.M.
- 1974. *Aspects of the Novel*. Harmondsworth: Penguin (1927)
Friedman, Norman
- 1955. 'Point of View in Fiction: The Development of Critical Concept.' *PMLA* 70, 1160–1184
Genette, Gérard
- 1969. 'Frontières du récit.' *Figures II*, Paris: Seuil
- 1972. *Figures III*. Paris: Seuil
- 1980. *Narrative Discourse*. Translated by Jane Lewin, with a Preface by Jonathan Culler. Ithaca: Cornell University Press
Glowínski, M.
- 1974. 'Der Dialog in Roman.' *Poetica* 8:1, 1–16
Greimas, A.J.
- 1966. *Sémantique structurale*. Paris: Larousse
- 1973. 'Les actants, les acteurs et les figures.' Cl. Chabrol et al., *Sémiotique narrative et textuelle*. Paris: Larousse
- 1976. *Maupassant: La sémiotique du texte: exercices pratiques*. Paris: Seuil
Greimas, A.J. and J. Courtés
- 1979. *Sémiotique. Dictionnaire raisonné de la théorie du langage*. Paris: Hachette
Hamon, Philippe
- 1972. 'Qu'est-ce qu'une description?' *Poétique* 1972

- 1977. 'Pour un status sémiologique du personnage.' R. Barthes et al., *Poétique du récit*. Paris: Seuil
- 1981. *Introduction à l'analyse du descriptif*. Paris: Hachette
- 1983. *Le personnel du roman*. Geneva: Droz

Hendricks, William O.
- 1973. 'Methodology of Narrative Structural Analysis.' *Semiotica* 7, 163–84

Hrushovski, Benjamin
- 1976. 'Poetics, Criticism, Science: Remarks on the Fields and Responsibilities of the Study of Literature.' *PTL* 1, iii–xxxv

Iser, Wolfgang
- 1978. *The Act of Reading: A Theory of Aesthetic Response*. Baltimore: Johns Hopkins University Press

Jakobson, Roman
- 1960. 'Closing Statement: Linguistics and Poetics.' Th. A. Sebeok, ed., *Style in Language*. Cambridge: MIT Press

Jefferson, Ann
- 1983. '*Mise en abyme* and the Prophetic in Narrative.' *Style* 17:2, 196–208

Kesteren, Aloysius van, and Herta Schmid
- 1975. *Moderne Dramentheorie*. Kronberg/Ts.

Kittay, Jeffrey S., ed.
- 1982. *Towards a Theory of Description*. New Haven (special issue of *Yale French Studies*)

Lämmert, Eberhard
- 1955. *Bauformen des Erzählens*. Stuttgart: J.B. Metzlersche Verlag

Lanser, Susan Sniaber
- 1981. *The Narrative Act: Point of View in Prose Fiction*. Princeton: Princeton University Press

Link, Hannelore
- 1976. *Rezeptionsforschung: Eine Einführung in Methoden und Probleme*. Stuttgart: Fink

Lodge, David
- 1977. 'Types of Description.' *The Modes of Modern Writing*. London: Edward Arnold

Lotman, Jurij M.
- 1977. *The Structure of the Artistic Text*. Ann Arbor: Michigan Slavic Contributions no. 7

McHale, Brian
- 1978. 'Free Indirect Discourse: A Survey of Recent Accounts.' *PTL* 3, 249–87

Pavel, Thomas
- 1976. *La synthaxe narrative des tragédies de Corneille*. Paris: Klincksieck; Ottawa: Éditions de l'université d'Ottawa

Pelc, Jerzy
- 1971. 'On the Concept of Narration.' *Semiotica* 2:3, 1–19
Perry, Menakhem
- 1979. 'Literary Dynamics: How the Order of a Text Creates Its Meanings.'
  Poetics Today 1:1, 35–64 and 311–61
Platz-Waury, Elke
- 1978. *Drama und Theater. Eine Einführung.* Tübingen: Max Niemeyer
  Verlag
Pratt, Mary Louise
- 1977. *Towards a Speech Act Theory of Literary Discourse.* Bloomington:
  Indiana University Press
Prince, Gerald
- 1973. *A Grammar of Stories.* The Hague: Mouton
- 1982. *Narratology. The Form and Function of Narrative.* The Hague:
  Mouton
Propp, Vladimir
- 1968. *Morphology of the Folktale.* Austin: University of Texas Press
Rimmon[-Kenan], Shlomith
- 1976. 'A Comprehensive Theory of Narrative: Genette's *Figures III* and the
  Structuralist Study of Fiction.' *PTL* 1, 33–62
- 1983. *Narrative Fiction: Contemporary Poetics.* London: Methuen
Ron, Moshe
- 1981. 'Free Indirect Discourse, Mimetic Language Games and the Subject of
  Fiction.' *Poetics Today* 2:2, 17–39
Schmid, Wolf
- 1973. *Der Textaufbau in den Erzählungen Dostoievskijs.* Munich: Wilhelm
  Fink Verlag
Souriau, Etienne
- 1950. *Les 200.000 situations dramatiques.* Paris: Larousse
Stanzel, Franz
- 1971. *Narrative Situations in the Novel.* Bloomington: Indiana University
  Press
Suleiman, Susan R., and Inge Crosman, eds.
- 1980. *The Reader in the Text.* Princeton: Princeton University Press
Tamir, Nomi
- 1976. 'Personal Narrative and Its Linguistic Foundation.' *PTL* 1:3, 403–30
Uspenskij, Boris A.
- 1973. *A Poetics of Comparison.* Berkeley: University of California Press
Walcutt, Charles C.
- 1966. *Man's Changing Mask: Modes and Methods of Characterization in
  Fiction.* Minneapolis: University of Minnesota Press

List of Definitions

Terms have been systematically provided with an explicit definition. This list refers to the pages where the definitions occur.